D0810783

THE
UNCONSCIOUS
CIVILIZATION

JOHN RALSTON SAUL

THE FREE PRESS

NEW YORK   LONDON   TORONTO   SYDNEY   SINGAPORE

THE FREE PRESS
A Division of Simon & Schuster Inc.
1230 Avenue of the Americas
New York, NY 10020

First Free Press Edition 1997
Previously published in Canada by House of Anansi Press Limited

THE FREE PRESS and colophon are trademarks
of Simon & Schuster Inc.

Manufactured in the United States of America

10 9 8 7 6 5 4 3 2 1

Library of Congress Cataloging-in-Publication Data

Saul, John Ralston.
    The unconscious civilization / John Ralston Saul.
        p. cm.
    Includes bibliographical references and index.
    ISBN 0-684-83257-7
    1. Corporate state.   2. Individualism.   I. Title.
JC478.S38   1997
330.1—dc20   96-41910
                                                        CIP

For
my parents

CONTENTS

I   The Great Leap Backwards   *1*

II   From Propaganda to Language   *39*

III   From Corporatism to Democracy   *74*

IV   From Managers and Speculators to Growth   *114*

V   From Ideology Towards Equilibrium   *154*

Notes   191

Acknowledgements   199

I

THE GREAT LEAP BACKWARDS

"WHO IS MORE CONTEMPTIBLE than he who scorns knowledge of himself?"[1]

A true question—a question seeking truth without expecting to find more than a fragment of it—will remain clear and unforgiving over hundreds of years. John of Salisbury raised this problem of self-knowledge in 1159. As you will see, much of what I'm going to say in these pages will be an amplification of his question.

John of Salisbury was far from the first to centre "the life worth living" on self-knowledge. What today we would call consciousness. Self-knowledge; the life worth living; individualism; humanism; a civil society. The list of terms describing the best and most interesting in the human experiment can be very long.

Not only was John of Salisbury not the first, he was surrounded in the twelfth century by a surprisingly large group of writers and thinkers, spread out across Europe—many of them monks or teachers—who were busy rediscovering the concept of the individual, perhaps even discovering for the first time what the modern Western individual could become if he, and later on she, wished.

Nowhere in all of this questioning, then or before, was the individual seen as a single ambulatory centre of selfishness. That idea of individualism, dominant today, represents a narrow and superficial deformation of the Western idea. A hijacking of the term and—since individualism is a central term—a hijacking of Western civilization.

One of the things I am going to do over these five chapters is describe that hijacking. The end result will be the portrait of a society addicted to ideologies—a civilization tightly held at this moment in the embrace of a dominant ideology: corporatism. The acceptance of corporatism causes us to deny and undermine the legitimacy of the individual as citizen in a democracy. The result of such a denial is a growing imbalance which leads to our adoration of self-interest and our denial of the public good. Corporatism is an ideology which claims rationality as its central quality. The overall effects on the individual are passivity and conformity in those areas which matter and non-conformism in those which don't.

Given the importance that John of Salisbury attributed to friendship and community, it is hard to imagine that he would not have asked the same question of society as a whole—particularly of ours, which is so determined to claim the individual as its anchor.

What is more contemptible than a civilization that scorns knowledge of itself?

I'll be more precise. It is taught throughout our universities, expounded in our think tanks, repeated *ad nauseam* in public forums by responsible figures—that democracy was born of economics, in particular of an economic phenomenon known as the Industrial Revolution. And that democracy is based upon individualism. And that modern individualism was also a child of the Industrial Revolution. (The less determinedly superficial of such voices will give some credit to the Reformation, which makes them only marginally less inaccurate.)

The point of these received wisdoms of the second half of the twentieth century is that the very heart and soul of our 2,500-year-old civilization is, apparently, economics, and from that heart flowed, and continues to flow, everything else. We must therefore fling down and fling up the structures of our society as the marketplace orders. If we don't, the marketplace will do it anyway.

The only problem with this whole theory is that much of modern individualism and democracy found life in Athens, some time before the Industrial Revolution. And both grew slowly, with ups and downs, through a series of key steps until the twelfth century, when the pace accelerated. Every important characteristic of both individualism and democracy has preceded the key economic events of our millennium. What's more, it was these characteristics that made most of the economic events possible, and not vice versa.

I'm going to come back to all of that later, but let me make one general point before moving on. Economics as a prescriptive science is actually a minor area of speculative investigation. Econometrics, the statistical, narrow, unthinking, lower form of economics, is passive tinkering, less reliable and less useful than car mechanics. The only part of this domain which has some reliable utility is economic history, and it is being downgraded in most universities, even eliminated because, tied as it is to events, it is an unfortunate reminder of reality.

Over the last quarter-century economics has raised itself to the level of a scientific profession and more or less foisted a Nobel prize in its own honour onto the Nobel committee thanks to annual financing from a bank. Yet over the same 25 years, economics has been spectacularly unsuccessful in its attempts to apply its models and theories to the reality of our civilization. It's not that the economists' advice hasn't been taken. It has, in great detail, with great reverence. And in general, it has failed.

A "profession" implies both real parameters and professionals who bear some responsibility for the effects of their advice. If economists were doctors, they would today be mired in malpractice suits.

That I even have to make this argument about the subsidiary nature of economics as it relates to individualism and democracy—and I'll come back to it later on to flesh out details—suggests that we are a dangerously unconscious civilization.

Not only do we seem to be devoid of useful memory, but when we do remember accurately it has little or no impact on our actions. It is as if, when we come to public action, our greatest desire is to generalize and institutionalize a syndrome resembling Alzheimer's disease. One-third to one-half of the population of Western countries is today employed in administering the public and private sectors. In spite of having a larger and better educated elite than ever before in history; in spite of knowing more than we have ever known about ourselves and our surroundings, we actively deny the utility of public knowledge.

In the nineteenth century, Alessandro Manzoni opened his great novel, *The Betrothed*, with one of those unforgiving resumés of our condition: "History may truly be defined as a famous war against time."[2] But you cannot wage this war if you deny reality. If you cannot remember, then there is no reality.

To know—that is, to have knowledge—is to instinctively understand the relationship between what you know and what you do. That seems to be one of our biggest difficulties. Our actions are only related to tiny, narrow bands of specialist information, usually based on a false idea of measurement rather than upon any knowledge—that is, understanding—of the larger picture. The result is that where a knowing woman or man would embrace doubt and advance carefully, our enormous, specialized, technocratic elites are shielded by a childlike certainty. Whatever they are selling is the absolute truth. Why link childishness to certainty? Quite simply, as Cicero put it: "He who does not know history is destined to remain a child."

There is little character difference between, say, Robert McNamara, maniacally convinced that the Vietnam War would, could, must be won or catastrophe would descend upon us—and he had the numbers to prove it—and the thousands of financial specialists maniacally convinced today that national debts will, can, must be paid off or catastrophe will swoop down upon us—and they have the numbers to prove it.

Let me give a small demonstration of this childlike state into which we are settling.

There is a general sense that our civilization is in a long-term crisis. It can be seen from the political or social or economic aspect. From each angle, the same crisis can be seen differently. I would argue that it took on its actual economic form in 1973, when a first wave of political crises led to an oil supply crisis. We have been in a depression ever since. It doesn't resemble a 1929-style depression, but then depressions have always been different, one from the other. Ours has been softened and evened out thanks to the life preservers gradually put in place by society after 1929 in order to give us time to manoeuvre and act should such a disaster repeat itself. It did, in 1973. Now, given our inability over the past two decades to deal with an unbreakable chain of unemployment, debt, inflation and no real growth, we have drifted farther and farther out into a cold, unfriendly, confusing sea. The new certitude of those in positions of authority—those out of the water—is that the certain answer is to cut away the life preservers.

This might be called a childlike act. Or one of unconsciousness so profound as to constitute stupidity.

How is this certitude possible? Well, the view from inside the public and private technocracy is one of relative calm. This is a place where the structure continues to grow, particularly in the private sector; particularly in the internationalized private sector. The technocracy has developed an argument that now dominates our society according to which "management" equals "doing," in the sense that "doing" equals "making." They have based this argument on a new economic mythology. This in turn is dependent on such things as the glorification of the service economy, a legitimization of financial speculation and the canonization of the new communications technology.

But of course, "managing" is neither "doing" nor "making." As Adam Smith put it: "There is one sort of labour which adds to the value of the subject upon which it is bestowed; there is another which has no such effect." The former is "productive," the latter "unproductive" labour. Smith clearly places management in the unproductive category. "The labour of some of the most respectable orders in the society is, like that of menial servants, unproductive of any value, and does not fix or realize itself in any permanent subject, or vendible commodity, which endures after that labour is past, and for which an equal quantity of labour could afterwards be procured."[3]

Smith, of course, is realistic: "But there is no country in which the whole annual produce is employed in maintaining the industrious. The idle everywhere consume a great part of it."[4] His argument is that the industrious produce the fund which finances the whole community. The idle—those not engaged in "useful labour"[5]—live upon the industrious. This includes the unwillingly idle—the unemployed. But he is not talking about them. They are not in a position to cost society a great deal.

He is referring above all to the managerial class of his

day—the aristocracy, the courtiers, the professionals, the land and property owners (who live off rent income), the bankers and so on. In other words, he is talking about our technocratic managerial elite. It must exist. But how much of it can the industrious among us support? The answer might be that 30 to 50 percent—the current level of the managerial class in our society—is far too high; that the management of business along with the financial and consulting industries—all of which are extremely expensive and increasingly so—are a far more important factor in keeping the economy in depression than is any over-expansion of government services.

Some of you will be surprised that I am invoking Adam Smith, the god of marketplace worshippers and of the neo-conservatives. Well, I am going to make a point of quoting both Smith and his friend David Hume, the demigod of the same contemporary Right, for two reasons. One is to show that the reigning ideologues of our day base their arguments upon a very narrow use of Smith and Hume. That they seriously misrepresent the more balanced message of the two men. And that the late industrial, global applications of Smith and Hume, which are now being pressed upon us, bear no relationship to the reality of what either man was talking about in an almost preindustrial and very localized situation.

Many are surprised that this management elite continues to expand and prosper at a time when society as a whole is clearly blocked by a long-term economic crisis. There is no reason to be surprised. The reaction of sophisticated elites, when confronted by their own failure to lead society, is almost invariably the same. They set about building a wall between themselves and reality by creating an artificial sense of well-being on the inside. The French aristocracy, gentry and business leadership were never more satisfied with themselves than in the few decades before their collapse during the French Revolution. The elites of the late Roman Empire were in constant expansion and filled with a sense of their own importance, as emperor after emperor was assassinated and provinces were lost. The Russian elites of the two decades preceding 1914—both the traditional leadership and the new, rapidly expanding business class— were in a constant state of effervescence.

One of the tricks which makes this sort of closet delusion possible is that the very size and prosperity of the elite permits it to interiorize an artificial vision of civilization as a whole. Thus, ours takes seriously only what comes from its own hundreds—indeed, thousands—of specialized sectors. Everything turns on internal reference. Everything is carefully measured, so that heartening "body counts" of growth or job creation or whatever can be produced. Truth is not in the world, it is the measurements made by professionals.

A few weeks ago I had a long conversation with the deputy minister of finance of a Western country. He allowed as to how many people outside—by which he meant outside the elite—believed that we were all caught up in a general, uncontrollable crisis. And that many attributed some of the blame to the international money markets, which were seen to have declined—through lunatic expansion—into a purposeless myriad of speculations upon repeated levels of paper unrelated to real production—unrelated, that is, to

Smith's "useful labour." The problem, the deputy minister said, was that each of these new money market mechanisms had its use within the financial system. Each was therefore useful. Not merely an exercise in speculation. He was, however, unable to relate this financial system to any broader idea of the economy or the society.

He also said that he himself had come from a poor family; that he had done well, as had his brothers and sisters. He therefore had difficulty believing that there was a crisis anywhere except at the margins of society. That his family's success might be related to the life preservers put in place after 1929—those protections against drowning that he and others were now cutting away—or that other people, not so fortunate as he and his family, might still need some help staying afloat, was beyond his interiorized, childlike vision of society.

The statistics of our crisis—which are available to all of us, as they are to this deputy minister—are clear and unforgiving. Yet they pass us by—in newspapers, on television, in conversations—as if they were not reality. Or rather, as if we were unable to convert knowledge into action.

I could recite a litany of these failures to you. Let me mention only a few, to illustrate the apparent meaninglessness of reality.

I'll begin with basics. Murder. Those of us who follow the phenomenon of war have watched while a handful of small conflicts in the early 1960s escalated to over 50 around the world today; all of them being fought concurrently; many of them major wars. The generally agreed statistics are that some 1,000 soldiers, and 5,000 civilians, die per day, every day, for a total of over two million deaths per year, for a total of 75 million deaths over the past 35 years. The conservative English military historian John Keegan states that 50 million people have been killed by war since the peace began in 1945.[6]

Either way these are record numbers. They make World War One into a sideshow. They make the Black Death into a small joke. In general, these deaths are not so much dismissed as eased off any serious agendas with the qualification that the wars in question take place mainly in the Third World. Whatever you think about that marginalizing qualifier, this has been less and less true since the end of the Cold War.

What's more, much of the responsibility for such violence lies with the international arms traffic—the largest international trade good of our day. It was launched in its modern form by the United States, France and then Britain in the early 1960s. Everyone else soon joined in. First the West, then the developing world. And when the Cold War ended, the promised peace dividend evaporated. The commerce in arms carried on at more or less the same levels. Today, a theoretically liberal American president has formalized a new campaign to increase the sale of weapons abroad, specifically as an arm of general trade policy.

We know all of this. But knowing seems to have no effect upon our unconscious.

Then there are the astonishing Third World statistics. Two hundred million children aged four to fourteen are in the work force. Life expectancy in Central Africa is 43 and dropping. One-third of the children in the world are undernourished. Thirty per cent of the work force is unemployed. The Third World debt crisis has not eased. That number is now some $1.5 trillion.

All of these numbers leave us confused, numbed, indifferent. This is knowledge with little effect.

What about focusing on a great case for hope? Mexico. On the basis of the assurances of the American and Canadian elites to their own citizens, Mexico was thrown into an increasingly unfettered North American trade arrangement. Mexico, we were told, was a developed democracy which, thanks to a reforming, free market president, had cleaned up its act and was capable of competing at our standards.

Scarcely two years later that president is suspected of involvement in the assassination of his chosen successor. A civil war has broken out in the south where 80 percent of the population earn less than $7 a day. Government-initiated torture, routinely denied by our elites two years ago, is now routinely admitted. After a revolutionary privatization of 80 percent of the state firms, the results are as follows. The state earned $21 billion, which instead of stabilizing the economy contributed to a massive economic collapse. On the positive side, some 30 billionaires were created—all friends of the president or the party in power. Unfortunately, if you weren't one of the 30 or one of their friends, real wages in Mexico plunged by 52 percent between 1980 and 1994. With much of the collapse of 1995 still to come, one-third of Mexican families were already living in extreme poverty. All of these figures are now far worse.

The knowledge of this misrepresentation of the Mexican situation by our elites has had no effect on the reality of American and Canadian policy. We are proceeding as if the illusion of two years earlier had been true.

And finally, what of the crisis inside the West itself?

The official Organization for Economic Cooperation and Development figure for unemployment in the West is about 35 million—that is, about 10 percent. This has not moved down seriously for a decade. This is also an unfinanceable level of exclusion for any society. In other words, no society can afford to lose the productivity of 10 percent of its population over an extended period of time. Nor can it afford to finance the lives of 10 percent of the working population, along with their families, left idle over an extended period of time. This figure of 10 percent is also, compared with our real levels of unemployment, a very low figure. Over the past two decades, the term "unemployment" has been redefined constantly—between 15 and 25 times in most Western countries—technical refinements, you understand—in order to eliminate certain categories or to create new categories. The purpose has been to keep the official statistics down. Rather than 35 million, the real unemployment figure is probably well over 50 million.

And although government after government, from the Left to the Right, has been elected on a platform of job creation, the reality is that they have no idea of what to do. Why? Because jobs are one of the last steps on the production chain. If you want jobs you must first research, develop, plan, risk, invest, build, develop markets and start selling. The result may eventually be jobs. But if you believe that the marketplace is in charge of all those functions—as the received wisdom of today assures us—well then, you shouldn't be promising jobs because you are abdicating any responsibility for the complex job-creating mechanisms. Anyway, the marketplace these days is into job elimination.

But our crisis isn't simply about jobs. The leader of the free world has 1.5 million people in jail: 373 citizens per 100,000. More than double what it was fifteen years ago. A rate second only to Russia. Put another way, 5.1 million Americans are in jail or under judicial supervision. Triple the figures of 1980.

The income of 75 million Americans is lower now than it was in 1966. Eighteen percent live under the poverty line. The inequality gap shrank continually between 1929 and 1969. Since then it has been continually widening. And not just in the United States. In most places. In the United Kingdom the gap between the highest and the lowest paid male workers is at its widest since 1880, when the compiling of statistics began. Edward Luttwak, the conservative American historian, says that if current trends continue, the United States will be a Third World country by 2020.[7]

Predictions are only predictions, but at least Mr. Luttwak is trying to conjure up the shape of the crisis. At least he is admitting that there *is* a profound crisis.

All of these numbers, and hundreds more of them referring to the same and to other countries, are well known. Yet the effect they have on real policy is negligible. In part this is because our elite is primarily and increasingly managerial. A managerial elite manages. A crisis, unfortunately, requires thought. Thought is not a management function. Because the managerial elites are now so large and have such a dominant effect on our education system, we are actually teaching most people to manage not to think. Not only do we not reward thought, we punish it as unprofessional. This primary approach to utility—a very limited form of utility—is creeping now into general pre-university education. The teaching of transient managerial and technological skills is edging out the basics of learning.

But there's another reason that knowledge of this crisis seems to have so little effect: the income of the elites at the upper levels has continued to grow and at the middle levels has not declined.

As Adam Smith put it, "The authority of riches . . . is perhaps greatest in the rudest age of society which admits of any considerable inequality of fortune."[8] By rudest, Smith means crudest, a term not often used to describe themselves by technocrats, specialists, managers and the professors at the Chicago School of Economics. Yet they do enjoy invoking Smith. Nor does "rudest" suggest a high level of civilization.

But what could be cruder than a human being, who is limited to a narrow area of knowledge and practice and has the naiveté of a child in most other areas? This is one of the elements that accounts for our clinical state of unconsciousness.

One of the related characteristics of this unconsciousness is the rise of illusion—in particular, the growth of fantastical descriptions of ourselves. For example, a number of neo-movements have developed over the past few years. People who want to be and yet not to be. The neo-fascists in Italy claim they are not fascists, yet 90 percent of their party members belonged to the old Fascist party. I have personally heard their leader, Gianfranco Fini, speak to a crowd of bankers, diplomats and politicians in London. He refused to condemn Mussolini. His policies were simply an updated, managerial-sounding version of Mussolini's, presented by someone who dressed and talked (I'm referring to his style) like a technocrat. He has said, "Italy has gone from an era in which nothing was known of politicians to one where they get photographed naked, as if they were actors. This is another sign that Italy has changed."[9] Well, actually it isn't. Mussolini was always photographed as if he were an actor. And behind Mussolini's flamboyant rhetoric was an obsession with modern management and corporatism. Fini dances to rock and roll in public, just as Mussolini prided himself on dancing in public to the latest tunes. These were then innovations in political style. Yet the illusion of being a neo has allowed Fini to escape from the shadow of fascism and gain substantial public power without abandoning his party's traditional policies.

The neo-corporatists have the same problem and even more success. The corporatist movement was born in the nineteenth century as an alternative to democracy. It proposed the legitimacy of groups over that of the individual citizen.

The first almost natural manifestation of this new way of governing came two centuries ago with the arrival of Bonaparte. Napoleon did more than invent modern Heroic leadership. He invented Heroic leadership which fronts for specialist groups and interest groups. Democracy and individual citizen participation were replaced by a direct, emotive relationship between the Heroic leader and the population. The new specialist, bureaucratic and business elites were thus left in peace to run things.

Hegel was one of the first to give this approach an intellectual form, as early as 1821, in *The Philosophy of Right*. The romantic revival of the medieval guilds was then under way in the guise of a 'natural link' between civil society and the state.

This early form of corporatism gradually emerged as the only serious alternative to democracy. It was increasingly proposed by the Catholic elites of Europe. They could accept the Industrial Revolution, so long as individualism was replaced by group membership. To the extent that individualism as citizen participation continued to exist, it was subjected to the limitations imposed by group membership. Many of these groups were apparently benign or even beneficial. Workers unions. Industrial owners associations. Professional associations. These corporations were not to function in conflict with each other. Through ongoing negotiations, they were to be nonthreatening and nonconfrontational bodies. Some of this system was formalized by Bismarck in the new Germany of the 1870s. But the corporatist alternative's moment of glory, so to speak, came half a century later under Mussolini and various other dictators, such as Portugal's Salazar.

The last thing today's neo-corporatists want is to be confused with these unpleasant dictators. Most of the intellectuals now involved in pushing this social formula are well-established university professors: political scientists, sociologists and economists, spread throughout the West. And yet, what they propose—the bald violence of the earlier generation aside—is virtually identical to the earlier model. They propose a basic shifting of legitimacy in our society from the citizen to the group. They don't put it quite that way. They talk modestly about facilitating the relationship between competing interest groups. The effect, however, would be far more profound than that.

In fact, I believe that we are already very close to having shifted the legitimacy inside Western society. Real power today lies with neo-corporatism, which is in fact old-fashioned corporatism.

The neo-conservatives, who are closely linked to the neo-corporatists, are rather different. They claim to be conservatives, when everything they stand for is a rejection of conservatism. They claim to present an alternate social model, when they are little more than the courtiers of the corporatist movement. Their agitation is filled with the bitterness and cynicism typical of courtiers who scramble for crumbs at the banquet tables of real power, but are always denied a proper chair.

The neo-fascists and neo-corporatists would like people to forget the content of their programs while they seek power. The neo-conservatives would like to pass themselves off as a movement of considerable historical importance, while working for something relatively short-term, self-interested and nasty.

Everything I've said so far revolves around an apparent inability to deal with reality. I would say that what we suffer from is a fear of reality. Who are "we"? Frankly, there is little difference in this mental state between those inside the elites and those outside. We have all by our actions or lack of them—in particular over the last quarter-century—agreed to deny reality.

The question is—Where does this fear come from? It isn't simply a vague taste for romantic illusions. We suffer from an addictive weakness for large illusions. A weakness for ideology. Power in our civilization is repeatedly tied to the pursuit of all-inclusive truths and utopias. At the time of each obsession we are incapable of recognizing our attitude as either a flight from reality or an embracing of ideology. The unshakeable belief that we are on the trail to truth—and therefore to the solution to our problems—prevents us from identifying this obsession as an ideology.

The history of this century—demonstrated in part by its unprecedented violence—suggests that our addiction is getting worse. We have already swept through the religion of world empires based upon the intrinsic superiority of each nation or race of empire builders, on through Marxism and Fascism, and now we are enthralled by a new all-powerful clockmaker god—the marketplace and his archangel, technology. Trade is the marketplace's miraculous cure for all that ails us. And globalization is the Eden or paradise into which the Just shall be welcomed on Judgement Day. As always with ideologies, the Day of Judgement is imminent and terrifying. I would suggest that Marxism, fascism and the marketplace strongly resemble each other. They are all corporatist, managerial and hooked on technology as their own particular golden calf.

Along with these great ideological passions, we have also suffered and continue to suffer from what might be called fashions—nationalization, privatization, debt financing, debt as the devil, the killing of inflation.

Fashion is merely the lowest form of ideology. To wear or not to wear blue jeans, to holiday or not to holiday in a particular place can contribute to social acceptance or bring upon us the full opprobrium of the group. Then, a few months or years later, we look back and our obsession, our

fears of ridicule, seem a bit silly. By then, we are undoubt-
edly caught up in new fashions.

But the wholesale, unquestioning embrace of political
policies does consist of more than wearing blue jeans. Each
of these miniature ideologies will disturb and often ruin
many lives. Each will also make the fortune of those who
wait patiently to feed off human credulity. Each, in the
oppressive air of conformity which ideologies create, will
force public figures to conform or be ruined on the scaffold
of ridicule. In a society of ideological believers, nothing is
more ridiculous than the individual who doubts and does
not conform. Think of the truisms of our day. Pay the debt.
Embrace globalization. Which public figure of which stripe
can stand up against these without committing political
suicide?

As a result, people like Tony Blair, leader of the British
Labour party, will go out of their way to fall into line. He
tells *The Financial Times* of London: "The determining context of economic policy is the new global market. That
imposes huge limitations of a practical nature—quite apart
from reasons of principle—on macroeconomic policies."[10]

These two sentences may sound familiar. They should.
They have been uttered in varying forms by hundreds of
public figures from the Right to the Left.

Globalization and the limits it imposes are the most fash-
ionable miniature ideologies of our day. Mr. Blair's statement means two things. One: 'I am in fashion so it's safe to
vote for me.' Two: 'The ideology is in charge, so don't worry,
I won't be able to do much.'

I myself would say that neither of these sentences is in

the least bit accurate. They are declarations of passivity before the inevitable—before what is said to be inevitable. This is a standard reaction to ideology. And passivity is one of ideology's most depressing effects. The citizen is reduced to the state of the subject or even of the serf.

There is a certain frightening dignity to the big ideologies. With the stroke of an intellectual argument the planet is put in its place. Terrifying. Only the bravest or the most foolish of individuals would not become passive before such awe-inspiring Destinies.

The minor ideologies, on the other hand, are almost always meanspirited and egotistical in the most straightforward way. They offer two choices—no more. And those two are really only one. Accept the ideology or perish. Pay the debt or go bankrupt. Nationalize or starve. Privatize or go moribund. Kill inflation or lose all your money. We have suffered from this 'either-or' sickness for a long time. In the Middle Ages, the scholastics at their worst summarized our choice as order versus disorder. Do what you are told or drop through the black hole. In 1995 the black hole is no longer a specific sin or a question of religious disobedience. But notice that the form of the argument remains religious and that passivity remains an expression of true belief.

I've talked about ideology and utopia as if they were one and the same. Is there no difference between them? Not really. Utopia is perhaps more of a literary term. But it expresses the real intent of the ideologue. Of course, no ideologue would be caught dead admitting to an utopian ideal. That would imply hope when what he is delivering is truth. He doesn't even see himself as an ideologue.

But why do we have this desperate need to believe that the solving of a single problem will solve all our problems? Or that a particular and absolute form of social organization will "bring history to an end"? "The need to fabulate," the French novelist Romain Gary said, "is just a child who refuses to grow up." "*Le besoin d'affabulation, c'est toujours un enfant qui refuse de grandir.*"[11]

Yet there is no innocent childish charm hidden within our need to fabulate; none, for example, in Professor Fukuyama's declaration that his side had won and therefore we had come to *The End of History*. Rather there was an unpleasant air of self-serving propaganda. Fabulation in all of us suggests a fear of reality. A weakness for ideology. A need to believe in single-stroke, cure-all solutions. A taste for the intolerance of conformity when we come to public policy. All of which translates into a debilitating passivity when faced by crises.

This suggests that we have difficulty perceiving our own weaknesses. Let me put this another way. If we are unable to identify reality and therefore unable to act upon what we see, then we are not simply childish but have reduced ourselves to figures of fun—ridiculous victims of our unconscious. The conscious human holds happily onto a sense of his own ridiculousness.

Unfortunately, our sense of the ridiculous in ourselves seems to ebb and flow, but to remain dangerously weak when it comes to public affairs. And the weaker it is, the more we tend to slip into an unhealthy, unconscious form of self-contempt. Worse still, we cultivate this loathing in our elites. We encourage them to think of us—the citizenry—with contempt, and so to think of themselves in the same way.

If we cannot see ourselves, then we cannot act as humans. It is hardly surprising that the result is a loss of self-respect.

This self-loathing is key to our weakness for ideology. Those who have the "truth" are by definition a small minority. They are the elect. Their desire is not to convince the rest of us of their truth. It isn't a matter of democratic debate with all the compromise that involves. They have the truth. The aim of the ideologue is therefore to manipulate, trick or force the majority into acceptance. People whom you intend to manipulate, trick or force are people for whom you have contempt. And if they, the majority, allow themselves to be taken in, well then, they do have contempt for themselves.

The modern version of this process first appeared during the Reformation—on both sides of the debate. The Protestants who accepted predestination accepted a profoundly passive existence for themselves. It is true that spreading the word was important, but good works would get them nowhere. God had already chosen who would be saved.

Everyone had but to wait for death to find out their ultimate destination. If, however, a small group could somehow convince itself that it knew the mind of God and that its members *were* the chosen few—the elect—well, then, they could throw off their passivity and drive the condemned majority before them. All and any methods were justified because the elect alone held the truth.

This was also the mentality of Ignatius Loyola and his Jesuits, who picked up the Protestant methods, thus adding a firm rational structure to Catholicism. Their intent was to give shape and weaponry to the Counter Reformation. Here was the beginning of modern ideology and absolutism.

The Jacobins of the French Revolution, the Bolsheviks, the Fascists, and now the free marketeers, are all the direct descendants of predestination and the Jesuits. They are the chosen few—the minority who have the truth and therefore have the right to impose it by whatever means.

Am I really being fair, throwing in among such a violent, bloody crew the market disciples, with their Chicago School of Economics *bona fides*, and their endless Nobel prizes, to say nothing of the neo-conservatives who are in general wonderfully educated?

Listen to Michael Oakeshott, the English philosopher, now dead, who is one of the father figures of the neo-conservatives. Politics, he said, is "vulgar," "bogus," "callous," because of the sort of people it attracts and "because of the false simplification of human life implied in even the best of its purposes."[12] Politics, he believes, should be left in the hands of men from the traditional political families, not some democratic, ambitious person.[13]

This same loathing for the majority can be found in the political philosopher Leo Strauss, who gave birth, in a sense, to Allan Bloom, who in turn, with great intelligence and style, demonstrated to the American public via his book *The Closing of the American Mind* that most of them were of an inferior nature. Intellectuals here and there followed suit. Botho Strauss, the well-known German playwright, wrote a trend-setting article in 1993 for *Der Spiegel* along somewhat the same lines.[14] He wrote it in a high literary German, incomprehensible to the majority of readers. Yet this elitism somehow inspired the rising groups of violent skinheads in Germany. Here is a vibrant example of self-hatred. The skinheads were inspired by an argument which, in its very form, denigrated them.

A little bevy of youngish Americans, mainly the sons of either rich or well-established families, has constituted itself as the North American branch of this movement. These are the eager courtiers of neo-conservatism. The atmosphere which reigns in their language is one of an embattled minority elite seeking ways to manoeuvre, manipulate and fool the majority into passive acceptance. In a recent public conversation they could be heard saying such things as:

"We can't really go to poor black people and throw them off welfare if we haven't first gone to rich white farmers and thrown them off welfare."

and

"The big programs, like welfare, Medicaid and Medicare, will take a little time to get rid of. But there are a lot of little ones that we can get rid of right away."

and

". . . it's dangerous for the Party to seem callous." (Note the word "seem.")

On the other hand:

"In the current environment being accused of callousness might even be to our advantage."[15]

Their air of cynical bitterness, in spite of their own comfortable situations, also suggests an unconsciousness of their own profound self-loathing. The tone throughout is one of religious sadomasochism. 'We have done wrong. We have had it easy. We indebted ourselves. Now we must pay. We must don hair shirts. We must impose suffering upon ourselves.' Of course, the suffering will fall on others, but that is beside the point.

The Italians have a wonderful word to describe a mummy's boy—*un mammone*. When I hear or read these people I can't help thinking of a daddy's boy. *Un pappone*. Someone who tries to be as tough as or tougher than his father.

In any case, their approach is pure Reformation politico-religious rhetoric. And like those church leaders 400 years ago, the new variety must, as the Canadian writer, M. T. Kelly, puts it, "create the other—the devil." This demonization is also essential to deny any "goodness or moral value to the other side."[16]

In fairness to the courtier tradition, it is important to add that by no means all of them have been, like the neo-conservatives, bitter and cynical. History is full of men and women who had to sing one tune or another for their supper. Often they had no choice if they wanted to play a public role. They were victims of the reigning social structure. Our society today is very much like that. The highly educated, technocratic, specialized elites who make up more than a third of our population are caught in structures which require of them courtier-like behaviour.

Today, as in history, their ranks are filled with people who try their best. They put up with the indignity of their role in order to eat—yes, we all must eat—but also in order to serve a good cause.

On the other hand, history also records a group of courtiers who have taken pleasure in the humiliation which their status demands. Often they were successful precisely because their self-loathing and cynicism allowed them to make the most of a situation that rewarded crude ambition and manipulation.

Shakespeare was particularly good at portraying the two types of courtiers, side by side. Inner strength versus weakness. An ethical centre versus vain ambition. A sense of the public good versus a wounded sense of having been personally wronged. Kent versus Edmund in *King Lear.* Rodrigo versus Iago in *Othello.*

The Iagos and Edmunds of our day are by no means limited to the ranks of neo-conservatism. As we gaze around at ministers' offices, at departmental administrations, at corporate executive suites, we can see courtiers of all sorts, making their way.

But the neo-conservative courtiers do appear to fall almost as a group into this category. Given that they are of age and legally responsible for their actions, this must be treated by society as a matter of their own choice.

Let me widen the focus here by briefly reintroducing the subject of corporatism.

First, corporatists from the 1870s on began laying in the idea that liberalism was guilty of a great sin because it had ". . . granted political and economic equality to individuals who were . . . manifestly unequal."[17] In other words, the corporatists were reviving the medieval hierarchical order.

Late in the century, the German, Max Weber, and the Frenchman, Émile Durkheim, gave corporatism a sophisticated intellectual shape. There were arguments over whether such a system should be state centred, economics centred, or society centred. But the only important point is that it was group centred and interest centred. The value of disinterest—that is in the sense of the disinterested act or the public good—was denied and ignored. The very idea of the public good was therefore vaporised.

In 1891, a papal encyclical—Retrum Novarum—came out against class struggle and proposed a modern version of the medieval scholastic dream of the perfect social order. This appeared to be a rejection of Marxist conflict in favour of 'social harmony.' In reality, it was a rejection of humanism, democracy, and responsible individualism in favour of administrative power sharing by interest groups.

After the First World War, men like Mihaïl Manoïlesco and Alfredo Rocco took these ideas further and prepared the antiparliamentarian atmosphere which led to a series of coups d'états and dictatorships in the 1920s and 1930s. With the arrival of Mussolini and a bevy of other dictators, corporatism found itself at the centre of modern power for the first time.

The underlying messages of Mussolini's system were efficiency, professionalism, management by experts, social order through ongoing group negotiations or what the neo-corporatists now call interest mediation. And all of this was to take place in a society balanced by Heroic leadership and market forces.

Contemporary corporatism has a more professional approach, and yet it is focused in an eerily familiar manner on training, meritocracy and organizational structures, which are inevitably pyramidal. In other words, the intent is exactly the same. This message is put out in a rhetorical, ideological manner through corporatism's mouthpieces—the disciples of market forces, the courtiers of neo-conservatism and, of particular importance, the authoritative voice of many social science academics.

Second, the denigration of such democratic, individualistic concepts as equality and justice has required from the very beginnings of corporatism a new set of social headings to put up over every doorway. This new approach was best evoked by Maréchal Pétain, the leader of collaborationist, corporatist France during World War Two. His slogan replaced *Liberté, Egalité, Fraternité* with *Patrie, Famille, Travail:* Nation (or rather, Fatherland), Family, Work. Other fascist, corporatist governments produced similar slogans.

Now, if you take a look at Newt Gingrich's list of "seven essential personal strengths for Americans," you will discover that 'work' is at the top of the list. 'Family' takes up four self-righteous variations on that theme in the middle. And at the bottom is an even more self-righteous version of 'nation.' Six out of seven comes pretty close. For that matter, three of his "Five Principles of American Civilization" deal with business, technology and organization—all characteristics of work. There is no mention of liberty or equality or, for that matter, of democracy. And that is because Gingrich is a fairly typical example of a corporatist who is disguised—at least in part unconsciously—behind the rhetoric of crude—that is to say false—individualism and false modernism.

But the arguments which will follow in these pages are not simply focused on our Western weakness for ideology. Or on our inability to recognize ideology as such when we are in its grip. Or on our resulting acceptance of a passivity that irritates us until we seek demons on the other side or a new ideology.

The larger question that intrigues me is whether or not we can ever escape this utopian nightmare. Remember, utopia is a word coined by Thomas More in 1516 from two Greek words: no + place. To live within ideology, with utopian expectations, is to live in no place, to live in limbo. To live nowhere. To live in a void where the illusion of reality is usually created by highly sophisticated rational constructs.

I am not, therefore, suggesting that we could escape to some pure and ideal future. That would be yet another ideology. But asking rather, how and to what extent can we escape ideology, even if it must be in a plodding, solid way. How can we limit the damage regularly wreaked by ourselves upon ourselves as the result of this apparently congenital weakness?

I am going to try to organize this conundrum into a series of oppositions. Real oppositions that involve real choices. Perhaps they should be called struggles. For example, humanism versus ideology. This could also be stated as balance versus imbalance or equilibrium versus disequilibrium.

As we go along, I'll come back regularly to these and other oppositions in order to enlarge upon them. What is humanism, for example? What could it be? And what do I mean by equilibrium? I'll devote much of the last chapter to that problem.

But even if I limit myself to the simple naming of these three parallel oppositions—ideology versus humanism; imbalance versus balance; disequilibrium versus equilibrium—you can sense that I am suggesting a more careful approach to ideas and policy. Such an approach might enable us, at least, to identify an ideology when we see one. In other words, we might be able to train ourselves to see the shapes of our own reality. And this might help us to be less easily made prisoner of the great inapplicable questions: What is civilization? What is man?

Ideologies always have the all-inclusive answer to these impossible questions. They phrase them a little differently, however—with the aggressiveness of assertion. What should civilization be? They know. What is man? Meaning, what he is leaves him with no choice.

Freed from these assertions we could fall back on more reasonable questions. What could civilization be? In practical terms, that is. What can humans realistically achieve and maintain for reasonable periods of time?

What I am suggesting may sound extremely simple. So simple as to be naive. I would remind you, however, that Socrates was executed not for saying what things were or should be, but for seeking practical indications of where some reasonable approximation of truth might be. He was executed not for his megalomania or grandiose propositions or certitudes, but for stubbornly doubting the absolute truths of others.

Let me slide the focus still wider. If I wanted to know what kind of society I was living in, I would begin by asking—Where does legitimacy lie? After all, the source of legitimacy is at the very heart of civilization. From that assumption about ultimate authority flows much of the rest: power, organization, attitudes both private and public, ethics admired or condemned or ignored. I can identify only four real options in Western history as the sources of legitimacy. A God. A King. Groups. Or the individual citizenry acting as a whole. There are many variations on these sources. Many kings have claimed direct inspiration from God and so combined the two. Modern dictators, from Napoleon on through Hitler, have claimed to inherit the legitimacy of a king. The groups have ranged from medieval guilds to modern corporatism.

Now, the peculiarity of the first three sources—God, king and the groups—is that, once in power, they automatically set about reducing the fourth, the individual, to a state of passivity. The individual citizen is reduced to the state of a subject. That is, he is subjected to the will of one or more of these other legitimacies.

In other words, gods, kings and groups are not compatible with the fourth source because they require acquiescence while individualism requires participation. Either one or more of the first three is in a dominant position or the fourth dominates.

I would argue that our society functions today largely on the relationship between groups. What do I mean by groups? Some of us immediately conjure up transnational corporations. Others think of government ministries. But this is to miss the point. There are thousands of hierarchically or pyramidally organized interest and specialist groups in our society. Some are actual businesses, some are groupings of businesses, some are professions or narrow categories of intellectuals. Some are public, some private, some well intentioned, some ill intentioned. Doctors, lawyers, sociologists, a myriad of scientific groups. The point is not who or what they are. The point is that society is seen as a sum of all the groups. Nothing more. And that the primary loyalty of the individual is not to the society but to her group.

Serious, important decisions are made not through democratic discussion or participation but through negotiation between the relevant groups based upon expertise, interest and the ability to exercise power. I would argue that the Western individual, from the top to the bottom of what is now defined as the elite, acts first as a group member. As a result, they, we, exist primarily as a function, not as a citizen, not as an individual. We are rewarded in our hierarchical meritocracies for our success as an integrated function. We know that real expressions of individualism are not only discouraged but punished. The active, outspoken citizen is unlikely to have a successful professional career.

What I am describing is the essence of corporatism. Forget the various declared intentions of the successive generations of corporatists—from the old Catholic groups to the Fascists to the spokesmen for pyramidal technocratic organizations to the well-intentioned neo-corporatist social scientists of today. What counts is what they have in common. And that is their assumption as to where legitimacy lies. In corporatism it lies with the group, not the citizen.

The human is thus reduced to a measurable value, like a machine or a piece of property. We can choose to achieve a high value and live comfortably or be dumped unceremoniously onto the heap of marginality.

To be precise: we live in a corporatist society with soft pretensions to democracy. More power is slipping every day over towards the groups. That is the meaning of the marketplace ideology and of our passive acceptance of whatever form globalization happens to take.

Our only serious reactions to this phenomenon have come in the form of angry populism, which I will argue later is largely false populism focused on such anti-democratic mechanisms as referenda and what is called direct democracy.

For the moment, I would like to expand on the particularity of gods, kings and groups. They cannot function happily within a real democracy—that is, within a society of individuals. They are systems devoid of what I would call disinterest. Their actions are based entirely upon the idea of interest. They are self-destructive because they cannot take seriously the long-term or the wider view, both of which are dependent on a measure of disinterest, which could also be called the public good or the common weal.

The society in which legitimacy lies with the individual citizen is quite different. It can happily tolerate gods, kings and groups, providing they do not interfere with the public good—that is, providing that they are properly regulated by the standards of the public good. The citizen-based society can do this because it is built upon the shared disinterest of the individuals. What's more, this has a tempering effect which can actually be beneficial to the other three forces— the gods, kings and groups. It limits their self-destructive nature by focusing them onto the longer term and the wider picture.

I believe that our ability to reassert the citizen-based society is dependent upon our rediscovery of the simple concepts of disinterest and participation. Both of these are a protection against our seemingly unconscious desire to take refuge in ideology. But the policies now being put in place throughout the West are based upon exactly the opposite assumption. Everything, from school education to public services, is being restructured on the self-destructive basis of self-interest.

I spoke earlier of three parallel oppositions or struggles—humanism versus ideology; balance versus imbalance; equilibrium versus disequilibrium. I can now add two more: democratic individualism versus corporatism; the citizen versus the subject. In the next chapter I'll deal with language versus propaganda and consciousness versus unconsciousness.

At this stage of our civilization, late in the twentieth century, I would say that we are losing each of these struggles to the darker side within us and within our society.

Am I exaggerating? Are we truly living in a corporatist society that uses democracy as little more than a pressure-release valve? Clearly the democratic mechanisms are still in place and the citizens do occasionally succeed in imposing a direction upon the elites.

But then, I am not making an absolutist argument. What I am talking about is the direction our society has taken. And how far it has gone along that path.

A simple test of our situation would involve examining the health of the public good. For example, there has never been so much money—actual money—disposable cash—in circulation as there is today. I am measuring this quantity both in absolute terms and on a per capita basis. Look at the growth of the banking industry and the even more explosive growth of the money markets.

There has never been so much disposable money, yet there is no money for the public good. In a democracy this would not be the case, because the society would be centred, by general agreement, on disinterest. In a corporatist system there is never any money for the public good because the society is reduced to the sum of the interests. It is therefore limited to measurable self-interest.

What then is the great leap backwards announced in the title of this chapter? It is our leap into the unconscious state beloved of the subject who, existing as a function in any one of the tens of thousands of corporations—public and private—is relieved of personal, disinterested responsibility for his society. He thus gives in to the easy temptation of embracing what I can only call the passive certitude offered by every ideology.

Let me close with two final oppositions. The first is that of permanent human patterns versus the temporary. Most of what is presented to us today as the inevitable forms of human relationships, given the dictates of such things as the market and technology, are in reality rather recent phenomena of a temporary—even incidental—nature. These are passing relationships because they are directly dependent upon the evolving forms of crude power. To develop theories about human nature and the nature of human society based upon temporary variations of this sort of power—as we have often done from Adam Smith on through Marx—is to waste a lot of time on the service roads of economics.

These phenomena can be seen in their truly ephemeral nature when compared to the essential propositions which have been with us virtually unchanged for 2,500 years. Solon's ideas of public justice; Socrates' view of the citizen's role as a persistent annoyance; Cicero's "The good of the people is the chief law";[18] John of Salisbury's "Who is more contemptible than he who scorns knowledge of himself?" There are thousands of other examples—in language and in action—of our efforts to improve ourselves by developing a responsible sense of self and society.

There is also a record of the ephemeral phenomena of self-interest. The trail is equally long—personal gain, violence for personal advancement, clever manipulation to get and hold power. The political figures who used their power for narrow purposes are often remembered, but generally as unfortunate examples of human weakness. The interesting thing is that nowhere in our active memory is this record of selfish acts in fact admired. It stands rather as a record of our failures.

This leads me to a final opposition. You might believe from the negative nature of my comments on us, the humans, that I myself am one of those who looks down contemptuously from the advantaged position of the elite and who therefore also suffers unconsciously from self-loathing.

But the confronting of reality usually is a negative process. It is ideology that insists upon relentless positivism. That's why it opposes criticism and encourages passivity.

I would argue that confronting reality—no matter how negative and depressing the process—is the first step towards coming to terms with it, which is what I will attempt to do in a small way over the next four chapters.

In this chapter I have simply been exercising my right as
a citizen—my Socratic right—to criticize, to reject conformity, passivity and inevitability. What encourages me in this
process is the "delight" that I take in the human struggle.[19]
Delight in mankind—that was the idea launched or rather
relaunched in the twelfth century by the forces of humanism
as they woke society from its Dark Ages.

The Roman poet, Terence, had said long before: "I am
human and nothing human is foreign to me." It was an attitude the humanists embraced in what they saw as a struggle
between delight and self-loathing—delight in your fellow
man and woman, sympathy for them; in other words, a
sense of society.

This was then as it is now a profoundly anti-ideological
idea which takes the human for what the human is and
believes it is worth trying to do better.

II

FROM PROPAGANDA TO LANGUAGE

I AM A SNAKE, not an apple.

What does that mean? Well, our civilization—the Judeo-Christian—in its founding myth portrayed the deliverer of knowledge as the source of evil—the devil—and the loss of innocence as a catastrophe. This probably had less to do with religion than with the standard desire of those in authority to control those who are not. And control of the Western species of the human race seems to turn upon language. Anyone who has worked with language, from the devil on, has been in the business of spreading knowledge. They are not knowledge itself. Novelists, playwrights, philosophers, professors, teachers, journalists have no proprietary right over knowledge. They do not own it. They may have some training or some talent or both. They may have a great deal of both. They will still be no more than the geniuses of dissemination.

That knowledge—once passed on as the mirror of creativity or as an intellectual argument or as the mechanisms
of a skill or as just plain information—may lead to increased
understanding. Or it may not. So be it.

Those of us who disseminate language are the snake not
the apple. What does this mean in a corporatist society
where knowledge is power—that is, in a society which
rewards and admires the control of information in its tiniest
fragments of specialization by the millions of specialists in
their thousands of corporations, public and private? The
apple is the game. Power, self-protection, self-advancement
are dependent on our ability to control knowledge as if we
were the apple itself. I would say we have now reached an
astonishing level of sophistication in our apple-envy psy-
chosis.

It is also worth noticing a curious characteristic of ideologies. They usually insist, in their justificatory argument, that
humans once lived in a happy, if somewhat crude or innocent, natural state. An Eden. By simply passing on through
the inevitable steps proposed by whatever particular ideology is in question, we are promised that we will re-enter
Eden at a higher, more sophisticated level. Paradise is the
first and the last destination. The origin and the end of the
human cycle.

Marx promised this. The Nazis promised this. And,
indeed, the market-forces ideologues promise this. Suffering
is inevitable in the short or medium term, but Paradise is the
next stop.

James Hillman, the American psychologist, asks repeatedly about the United States:

"Why are we a culture that doesn't want to lose its innocence?"

"What is the moral superiority of being innocent?"

"Why are sophistication and culture somehow corruption?"[1]

Many elements no doubt contribute to this syndrome. But it is worth noticing that the heart of market ideology beats in the United States and that the believers preach two contradictory visions: (1) a return to the American small-town ideal; (2) the achievement of a magic balance that will be created by the freeing of the capitalist mechanism. Most sensible people would be surprised by the suggestion of such a strange cohabitation. The global economy and the small-town ideal are not simply nonsequiturs. They are direct enemies. But there is no need for the sensible in a utopia.

For the ideologue, language itself becomes the message because there is no doubt. In a more sensible society, language is just the tool of communication.

The role of the writer is to force the pace of communication. To flee conformity and courtierism. Socrates in the *Apology*, his defence argument during his trial, said that he had no choice but to go through the streets, philosophizing, "examining himself and others." He took on—and thus annoyed—everyone from merchants to children. There is no difference between this and, for example, the great German novelist Heinrich Böll's unceasing criticism of the *nouveau riche* in postwar Germany and of, as Gordon Craig has put it, "a callous and bureaucratized society that believed only in power, influence and money."[2]

The important thing in the role of the writer is the maintenance of independence. Some may become tied to political
causes. This can be a success or a disaster. Witness Mon-
taigne advising Henri de Navarre, and so playing an important role in the declaration of the Edict of Nantes, one of the
first formalizations of modern religious freedom.[3] On the
other hand there is the philosopher Martin Heidegger, university chancellor, in a Nazi uniform, declaring that Hitler
and the Germans were "guided by the inexorability of that
spiritual mission that the destiny of the German people
forcibly impresses upon history."[4]

What Socrates and Böll were delivering was knowledge
that fosters doubt. And doubt is central to a citizen-based
society; that is, to democracy.

One of the best descriptions I've read of this role again
came out of that postwar Germany trying to find itself in the
self-induced wreckage—not just physical, but moral and
cultural—of what a few decades earlier had been its civilization. Walter Jens wrote:

> The German writer of our day, representing no class,
> under the protection of no fatherland, allied with no
> power, is . . . a threefold lonely person. But it is pre-
> cisely . . . this freedom from ties, that gives him a terri-
> ble, unique opportunity to be free as never before. . . .
> In a moment when blind obedience rules, the No of the
> warner, the Erasmian hesitation, reflection and Socratic
> caution are more important than ever.[5]

What then, as I asked a few moments ago, does all of this

mean in a corporatist society? In our society, that is? I would say, first, that the role of the writer—and of language—is more tenuous today than it has been since the late Middle Ages.

True, there have never been so many writers, so many books, such a babble of language flowing around us via so many new communication devices. And more language-distributing technology arrives in the public place every day.

Yet in a corporatist society, most people in positions of responsibility—public or private—are rewarded for controlling language. "Knowledge is Power." That is the bold headline advertising a conference organized by *The International Herald Tribune.* They promise that heavyweights from the public and private sectors around the world will be present. This will be an opportunity to make "contacts," make "a deal." "Most of all, you acquire the knowledge that just may give you the edge on your competition."[6] "Acquire" is used here in its financial sense. Knowledge is owned and controlled, bought and sold, in a corporatist society— knowledge which matters, that is.

The people who have it, do have power as we understand power today, given our managerial, technocratic elite. Knowledge is one of the currencies of systems men, just as it was for the courtiers in the halls of Versailles. They require a position in the structure that provides them with some ability to deny access to others and gain access for themselves. Then they require currency or chips to play the systems game. That is, they need information.

When our elites do not resemble these royal courtiers, they are reminiscent of the schoolmen of the late Middle

Ages whose profession was to tie down debate in minutiae as a way of making themselves relevant to power. The schoolmen came to believe that they were the apple itself.

But what about that astonishing babble of language which inundates us every day—particularly via information technology—everything from radio and television to the latest computer breakthrough? Frankly, if it doesn't relate in some practical way to the structures of power, then it is just so much babble. The most remarkable steam-release device ever to have existed.

I don't want to exaggerate. If an enormous public effort is made to use this babble for a specific cause, it can, from time to time, have some effect on power. But compare these small and short-lived victories with what happens when the corporatist power structures use those same systems. The ratio of their success in heading off citizen opposition to the dominance of group interests is probably 100 to 1 against the babble; 100 to 1 for corporatism and against democracy.

I'll go further. In the eighteenth century it was believed by the Enlightenment thinkers that access to knowledge would create unbeatable arguments against doing wrong. These affirmations of truth were to be aimed at the powers of the day—the church and the monarchy. Today's power uses as its primary justification for doing wrong the knowledge possessed by its experts. They know, therefore, that they must do whatever is necessary. This is how hospitals are closed or public education is squeezed or taxes shifted from those who have to those who have less. Knowledge is more effectively used today to justify wrong being done than to prevent it.

This raises an important question about the role of freedom of speech. We have a great deal of it. But if it has little practical effect on reality, then it is not really freedom of speech. Without utility, speech is just decorative.

The corporatist structures have been remarkably successful at limiting this utility. The actions of the private sector are obscured in a world made increasingly opaque by the unending quantities of information—that is, of rhetoric and propaganda—which shower down on those outside the interest groups. As for the freedom of information or access to information laws, they have simply confirmed that all information is private unless it is specifically requested. Requests must be clearly defined and often cost money, with the result that information is stored in increasingly narrower and more specific categories. A request produces a fragment of information, and only those citizens with funds can engage in these frustrating fishing expeditions.

Those who believe that democracy issued from the womb of the marketplace have a tendency to link freedom of speech to capitalism. George Bush, for example, in his inaugural address spoke of how a "more just and prosperous life for men on earth" was accomplished through "free markets, free speech and free elections." The order given to the three freedoms is astonishing from the mouth of a man assuming the chief responsibility for the exercise of the American constitution. His suggested sequence of freedoms is an historical and contemporary fiction. The world is filled today, as it has often been in the past, with nations that embrace free markets, close censorship and false or no general elections.

Singapore and China spring to mind. And the more complete these markets, the tighter the controls become on the other two freedoms.

Finally, free speech and democracy are closely tied to an active, practical use of memory—that is, history—as well as an unbroken sense of the public good. Commerce has no memory. Its great strength is its ability to constantly start again: a continual recreation of virginity. Commerce also has no particular attachment to any particular society. It is about making money, which is just fine, as far as it goes.

The reality, available to any of Mr. Bush's speech writers, is that freedom of speech was clearly and consciously identified for the first time as an essential element of democracy around 470 B.C. That, I believe, is 2,250 years before the Industrial Revolution. Aeschylus, the earliest of the great Athenian poet-playwrights, talks in the *Suppliants* of the free tongue as an essential democratic element. This was 70 years before Socrates' death. The concept appears to have been commonly accepted. And the Greek writers played their role in solidifying this link because they filled in their plays with the arguments going on in the streets and the assemblies.

Like so many of society's great victories, freedom of speech was easier to lose than to win. And so it has had to be constantly reconquered and maintained. Gustave Flaubert, whose *Madame Bovary* survived an attempt to have it seized, wrote that "censorship, whatever it is, seems to me to be a monstrosity, something worse than murder; an assassination attempt on thought; a crime of *lèse-âme* [*lèse*-soul, as in *lèse-majesté*]. The death of Socrates still weighs on the human species."[7]

Leonardo Sciascia in his novel *The Council of Egypt* describes a viceroy of Sicily in the nineteenth century who expresses in a conversation the perpetual attitude of authority towards freedom of speech. In Sicily, this attitude could easily be transformed into reality:

> And these books, this plague of books, you have no idea of the number, of how many copies of each get here: by the box-load, by the cart-load. . . . Still, as many as arrive, as many are burnt by the state executioner.[8]

But in a corporatist society there is no serious need for traditional censorship or burning, although there are regular cases. It is as if our language itself is responsible for our inability to identify and act upon reality.

I would put it this way. Our language has been separated into two parts. There is public language—enormous, rich, varied and more or less powerless. Then there is corporatist language, attached to power and action. Corporatist language itself breaks down into three types. Rhetoric, propaganda and dialect. I'll come back to rhetoric and propaganda later on. For the moment let's concentrate on dialects. Not the old-fashioned regional dialects, but the specialized, inward looking verbal mechanisms (I'm avoiding the word language because they are not language; they do not communicate) of the tens of thousands of monopolies of fractured knowledge. These are what I would call the dialects of the individual corporations. The social science dialects, the medical dialects, the science dialects, the linguist dialects, the artist dialects. Thousands and thousands of them, purposely impenetrable to the non-expert, with thick defensive walls that protect each corporation's sense of importance.

The arts cannot blame business for this phenomenon— anymore than business can blame the arts, or either of them blame or be blamed by public servants or scientists. The reliance on specialist dialects, indeed the requirement to use specialist dialects, has become a universal condition of our contemporary elites.

But the core of this disease is perhaps to be found in the social sciences. These often well-intentioned, potentially useful false sciences, feed the dialects of the public and private sectors. The humanities themselves are increasingly infected by both the social science method and its approach to language.

Over-compensation is one explanation for this. Economists, political scientists, and sociologists in particular have attempted to imitate scientific analysis through the accumulation of circumstantial evidence, but, above all, through their parodies of the worst of the scientific dialects. As in business and governmental corporations, the purpose of such obscure language could be reduced to the following formula: Obscurity suggests complexity which suggests importance. The dialects are thus more or less conscious weapons of self-protection and unconscious tools of self-deception.

This splitting of language into a public domain versus a corporatist domain makes it very difficult for anyone— outsider or insider—to grasp reality. Without a language that functions as a general means of useful communication, civilizations slip off into self-delusion and romanticism, both of which are aspects of ideology, both aspects of unconsciousness.

Of all centuries for this to happen! The explosion in every level of education and the arrival of the Freud–Jung duo ought to have brought us, perhaps for the first time, close to our best as conscious humans—functional not dysfunctional, eager to spread knowledge and understanding.

"Consciousness is a precondition of being," Jung announced.[9] He saw this very clearly in the context of what I described in the first chapter as our self-loathing.

> It is astounding that man, the instigator, inventor and
> vehicle of all these modern developments, the origina-
> tor of all judgements and decisions and the planner of
> the future, must make himself such a *quantité néglige-*
> *able.* The contradiction, the paradoxical evaluation of
> humanity by man himself, is in truth a matter for won-
> der, . . . springing from an extraordinary uncertainty of
> judgement—in other words, man is an enigma to him-
> self. . . . He knows how to distinguish himself from the
> other animals in point of anatomy and physiology, but
> as a conscious, reflecting being, gifted with speech, he
> lacks all criteria for self-judgement.[10]

Perhaps the difficulty with the psychoanalytic movement is that from the beginning it has sent out a contradictory message: Learn to know yourself—your unconscious, the greater unconscious. This will help you to deal with reality. On the other hand, you are in the grip of great primeval forces—unknown and unseen—and even if you do know and see them, it is they who must dominate. "Called or not," as the sign over Jung's door said, "the gods will come."

It's not that Freud and Jung lacked genius or were insufficiently careful in their selling of the benefits of their breakthrough. They were extremely careful. Ivan Klima, the Czech writer, talking about the more general question of historical and social habit, put the difficulty of the situation very well. "It would be naive to believe that the forces determining human behavior for centuries have been tamed because we have, in part at least, determined what they are and named them."[11] Klima's point is that naming these forces is just the beginning of a difficult and permanent struggle.

The Freud–Jung problem, however, is quite different. As James Hillman and Michael Ventura put it, half seriously, *We've Had a Hundred Years of Psychotherapy and Things Are Getting Worse.*[12]

Although Jung went out of his way to warn against mistaking narrow self-knowledge for consciousness, much of the attraction of the movement has come from the possibility of gaining what I would call a sense of false individualism.

Jung warned: "Most people confuse 'self-knowledge' with knowledge of their conscious ego-personalities." "What is commonly called 'self-knowledge' is therefore a very limited knowledge."[13] Or, more brutally, "Since it is universally believed that man is merely what his unconsciousness knows of itself, he regards himself as harmless and so adds stupidity to iniquity."[14]

In this century, dominated by mass ideologies, all-inclusive structures and technological revolution, it is as if the Western individual has taken refuge in the search for something that no one can take away—their own unconscious. Therapy, as Hillman puts it, thus becomes yet another ideology—"a salvational ideology."[15] But this flight into the unconscious has gone far beyond formal therapy into the general Western myth of what an individual is and—more importantly—what properly should interest an individual. The answer? Himself. Herself. Not society. Not civilization. The particular versus the whole. The narrowly examined life of the passive citizen versus the unexamined life of the twentieth century.

The other misfiring of the Freud–Jung breakthrough has been the effect on society of its use of the eternal myths. We think of Jung in particular as being concentrated on the Gods and Destiny. But Freud's obsession was only slightly different. Sex, the Gods and Destiny.

Why am I going on about this? Because the Gods and Destiny are the two central characteristics of all ideologies. They are called different things by each new faith. But they are the totems of inevitability.

Western civilization properly began two-and-a-half millennia ago, when thinkers such as Solon and Socrates broke the Homeric myth according to which the Gods and Destiny ruled all. The message Homer sent out was that no matter how intelligent, strong, talented or beautiful you were, your life was predetermined by the Gods and Destiny.

Listen to Homer's approach in *The Iliad*.

Agamemnon to Achilles:
What if you are a great soldier—who made you so but God?

Hector to his wife:
But Fate is a thing that no man born of woman, coward or hero, can escape.

Patroclus to Achilles:
Is it possible that you are secretly deterred by some prophecy, some word from Zeus that your lady Mother has disclosed to you?

Hector to Glaucus:
We are all puppets in the hands of Zeus.[16]

Homer builds his story upon hundreds and hundreds of these inevitabilities. Before the questioning of civilization began 2,500 years ago in Greece, his stories were received not as fiction or myth or history, but rather in the way Biblical text was received at the height of the Christian era. It was treated as literal truth. The great escape from the Gods and Destiny—the escape that made Western civilization possible—was based on the growing conviction that the human race, within the limits of reality, could give direction to its society, just as individual citizens within that society could give direction to their lives. It is our constant awareness of those limitations imposed by a myriad of concrete factors which saves us from the absolution of ideology and the resulting disasters. When we go off the rails it is often because we have forgotten that small but essential clause—"within the limits of reality."

But now, in this century of ideologies, the Gods and Destiny have been given new life. "Miracles in the world are many," Sophocles wrote in the fifth century B.C. "There is no greater miracle than man." Suddenly, at the end of the twentieth century, we discover that no, after all, it isn't true. Historical inevitability is a greater miracle than man. As is the dialectic. As is the superiority of various groups according to blood type. As is the genius of an abstract mechanism called the market. As is the leadership of inanimate objects—called technology—which worker bees create and then, inevitably, are led by.

These inevitabilities are great leaps backward into the arms of the Gods and Destiny. I'm not suggesting that Freud and Jung intentionally threw us back into this lower form of human life. In a sense they were the inevitable, confused voice of a century that saw abstract rational egocentrism crash on the rocks of reality with indescribable and unprecedented violence. At a time when people feel betrayed or abandoned by their civilization, they have been presented with an explanation of their sense of impotence: the archetypes, the eternal myths, the unchangeable. Instead of giving them a new sense of power, the explanation gives comfort to passivity—particularly public passivity—faced with the reigning ideologies.

There is one area in which there is some concrete blame to be assigned. In an era that saw the rise of dangerous individuals—modern versions of the Hero—Jung was not careful enough in how he described his archetypes. He talks, for example, about the road to consciousness, ridding ourselves of what possesses us, developing a complex free ego. But then he describes that ego. It would "be assured of an impregnable position, the steadfastness of a superman or the sublimity of a perfect sage. Both figures are ideal images: Napoleon on the one hand, Lao-tzu on the other."[17]

Napoleon: the first modern dictator, the first exploiter of rational absolutism, the subverter of democracy, initiator of modern Heroic propaganda, the model for every twentieth-century dictator from Hitler and Mussolini on. It is difficult to see how a sensible thinker could advance Napoleon as an ideal image for the conscious human. In fact, Jung's models can and, in an unconscious sense have, I think, been taken as a further development of the Hero-worshipping laid out by Thomas Carlyle in the nineteenth century. Carlyle, like Jung, threw the military dictators together with the sages. They were not, he argued, qualitatively different. They were simply different facets of the heroic personage. In Carlyle's case, he was advertently providing intellectual legitimacy for the anti-democratic movements that would follow. The remarkable strength of ideologies in the twentieth century is, at least in part, due to his efforts.

Advertently or inadvertently, the work of the psychotherapists has also helped legitimize the rise of both the modern ideologies and the modern Heroes. You can see this trend in the work of a disciple like Joseph Campbell. Freud and Jung set out to conquer the unconscious. However, by sending us back into the arms of the Gods and Destiny, they may instead have pushed us to cling hysterically onto the unconscious.

It is as if our obsession with our individual unconscious has alleviated and even replaced the need for public consciousness. The promise—real or illusory—of personal self-fulfillment seems to leave no room for the individual as a responsible and conscious citizen.

The apparent corollary of the psychoanalytic movement's drive for personal consciousness is an unconscious civilization. What Jung probably imagined would produce a marriage of the inner and the outer life of the individual alone and as citizen has instead produced an either/or situation.

Of course, misinterpretation or inadvertent interpretation is the great fear of writers who have any sense of the real world into which their language flows. Perhaps that is why so many of the key thinkers—let me call them the conscious thinkers—have feared the written word and expressed themselves through the oral. Socrates, Christ, Francis of Assisi are obvious examples. Shakespeare's plays were almost oral, written down in bits and pieces, changed repeatedly on stage. Even many who wrote—Dante, for example, or the great figures of the Enlightenment—consciously sought to use a language polished into a simple clarity that could both evoke the oral and be used as if it were oral.

Harold Innis, the first and still the most piercing philosopher of communications, wrote a great deal about the problem of the written or what George Steiner calls "the decay into writing."[18]

The deeper we go into the written, the deeper we go into mistaking the snake for the apple—the messenger for the message. I've said before that one of the signs of a healthy civilization is the existence of a relatively clear language in which everyone can participate in their own way. The sign of a sick civilization is the growth of an obscure, closed language that seeks to prevent communication. This was increasingly the case with those medieval university scholars known as the schoolmen. This is the case today with those who wield the thousands of impenetrable specialist dialects. They plead complexity, given this century's great advances, particularly our technological breakthroughs. But the problem is not one of complexity. Not many outsiders actually want to know the nuts and bolts of building jumbo jets or writing post-modern novels. It is the intent that is in question—the intent to use language to communicate, or alternately, through control of it, to use language as a weapon of power.

Unconsciousness—even hysterical unconsciousness—is not a surprising characteristic in a corporatist society where the language attached to power is designed to prevent communication.

"A life without this sort of examination is not worth living," Socrates said in the most famous sentence of his trial defence. He was referring to the ongoing self-examination that public philosophy involved. And philosophy is a matter of public debate or it is nothing. Philosophy as just another specialist corporation is a flagrant return to medieval scholasticism.

Socrates' idea of self-examination was by no means an isolated thought in the two-and-a-half millennia separating the first of Western history's two key trials from the revelations of Freud and Jung. The wonderful twelfth-century disinterrers of real individualism were almost obsessed by this problem.

Aelred of Rievaulx asked: "How much does a man know,

if he does not know himself?" and St. Bernard wrote to Pope Eugenius: "Begin by considering yourself—no, rather end by that." Peter Abelard wrote a book called *Ethics or Know Yourself*.

None of these people was referring to our goofing-off versions of individualism or to our increasing self-absorption. Their concepts do not arise from economics or eternal unchangeable myths. They saw the individual as a reality in a community of friends within a society.

Why, you may wonder, do I repeatedly, in this reflection on the twentieth century, reach back to the twelfth, and even beyond, to Socrates? Is this an intellectual fetish?

I would explain it this way. What does not change in human relationships are the basic choices that repeatedly face us. Those basic choices can be affected by material conditions, but they are neither created nor destroyed by them.

The basic opposition that lays out most of these choices was put in place during the heyday of Athens. It was and remains the opposition between Socrates and Plato. Socrates—oral, questioner, obsessed by ethics, searching for truth without expecting to find it, democrat, believer in the qualities of the citizen. Plato—written, answerer of questions, obsessed by power, in possession of the truth, antidemocratic, contemptuous of the citizen. Socrates, the father of humanism. Plato, the father of ideology. Plato's greatest flaw is also the secret of his ongoing political success. He managed to marry Homer's inevitability of the Gods and Destiny to the newly discovered mechanisms of reason.

Now, you don't often hear this argument because Plato, having written so much of Socrates, succeeded in confusing himself with the great martyr. And he did so to the advantage of his own arguments. As a result, Socrates seems at times a democrat, at other times anti-democratic. Sometimes he's in the streets, obviously enjoying his verbal duelling matches with citizens; sometimes he is at aristocratic dinner parties making insulting elitist remarks about the citizenry.

The result is that the Platonists, with their fundamental belief in authoritarianism justified by high intelligence and high learning, have been able to count Socrates more or less as one of their own. Worse still, they have been able to cite Socrates' trial and execution as proof that democracy is a base affair and the citizens contemptible.

For those who took the time it was always possible to disentangle the two philosophers. Confusion remained in the language because of the single author, but Socrates' actions indicated where he actually stood.

However, a recent book by Gregory Vlastos has now removed all the confusion. *Socrates: Ironist and Moral Philosopher*[19] is one of the most important pieces of scholarship of our time. It is a great and valuable tool for the communication and understanding of our basic Western argument. Vlastos has taken all of the Socratic texts and broken them down into ten theses over three periods. He demonstrates that the early Socrates is either in disagreement with the middle and later Socrates, or is simply dealing with different matters. It becomes clear that the early Socrates was a reasonably faithful rendering of the master's ideas by Plato, the then-impressionable young disciple. The two later periods are the mature Plato himself, using Socrates as a dramatic persona—a front, if you like—for his own ideas.

The early Socrates is a populist, the later an elitist. The early seeks knowledge while avowing he has none, the later seeks demonstrative knowledge and is sure he finds it. The early prefers Athens' system to any other, the later ranks democracy as one of the worst forms of government. In that same context, Books II to X of *The Republic* propose a complex utopia—the model of what would become modern ideology. However, the first book, the earliest, does no such thing.

In Vlastos' words, "As Plato changes, the philosophical persona of his Socrates is made to change, absorbing the writer's new convictions, arguing for them with the same zest with which the Socrates of the previous dialogues had argued for the views the writer had shared with the original of that figure earlier on."[20]

What does all of this mean for us in the late twentieth century? Well, it means that the humanist, individualistic, democratic argument has come to us in a direct, unimpeded line from the very first century of our civilization. With each successful expression of this argument over the centuries the language is clear, the idea of the disinterested public good is reinforced, the citizen is identified as the source of legitimacy. And this ethical, humanist, democratic line stretches across 2,500 years, free and independent of the evolving specifics of economics, technology, intellectual elitism and military force, among other periodic expressions of the Western experience.

In Socrates' own words, his goal is "to determine the conduct of our life—how each of us should conduct himself to live the most advantageous life." "What is the way we ought to live?" "Let no day pass without discussing goodness."

In opposition to all of this we can also get a clear view of Plato and the Platonists—as varied a bunch over the millennia as the humanists. By simply reading *The Republic* (from Book II on, that is), we find the original model of the corporatist utopia that is being pressed upon us today. In the Middle Ages we find Plato's philosopher-king being mixed into Christianity to produce the absolute monarch.[21] We find that same philosopher-king elitism in the thinkers of the current neo-conservative movement. As Vlastos points out, the Socratic "say what you believe" turns into the Platonic "purely instrumentalist conception of justice." We can understand through the Platonic past the uncomfortable silence of our elites today and their Hobbesian taste for law, not as justice, but as contract and fear. We can see and know that the Platonists are in power.

The Socratic–Platonic opposition can be used in yet another way. The young disciple, Plato, was bitter over his master's conviction and execution. But let us ask an irresponsible question. If Plato had been Socrates' age in 399 B.C.— that is, 70 years old—and had been chosen for that jury of 501 citizens, how would he have voted? Of course I have no idea. What we do know is that by the age of 70 Plato, a great genius, had turned into a vendor of utopias, an absolute answerer of absolute questions, elitist and authoritarian— fond of order and contemptuous of citizens' rights; contemptuous, that is, of the legitimate doubter in a democracy.

Socrates, on the other hand, had reached 70, and his trial, full of ironic humour, questions and a terrifying consciousness. He was a force of doubt and thus of disorder, from the utopians' point of view.

The evidence suggests that Plato might have had difficulty casting a not-guilty vote.

This irresponsible question is an interesting one to ask of ourselves. Or to ask of those who seek to guide us. How, for example, would Allan Bloom have voted? Michael Oakeshott? Who among the leaders of our elites does not fear living with the conscious realization that they do not know? If they are driven by that fear, which encourages their addiction to answers—or rather to solutions, as we call them now—how would they have voted?

This is perhaps the right moment to go back to my analysis of language broken into two parts—the public and the corporatist. And the corporatist language itself broken into rhetoric, propaganda and dialect—the three ideological tools used for preventing communication.

It is difficult to separate the first two. Rhetoric describes the public face of ideology. Propaganda sells it. They are both aimed at the normalization of the untrue. Earlier I quoted George Bush's inaugural address: "We know how to secure a more just and prosperous life for man on earth: through free markets, free speech, free elections." As I pointed out, this statement is both inaccurate and the elements in it out of order. Yet, the identical rhetoric can now be heard flowing effortlessly out of other governments with other political persuasions. The Liberal government in Canada declared in its 1995 foreign policy statement—as if it were an obvious truth—that "human rights tend to be best protected by those societies that are open to trade, financial flows, population movements, information and ideas about freedom and human dignity."[22] Again, this is demonstrably inaccurate. Many dictatorships are open to trade, financial flows and population movement. But above all, note again the preposterous order, with freedom tacked on at the tail end of a long list designed to describe the protection of human rights. This sort of rhetoric is in the same category as the words I have already quoted from Tony Blair: "The determining context of economic policy is the new global market . . ." and so on.

The modern origins of this sort of verbiage is the formal Jesuitical rhetoric of the sixteenth century. Its aim was to gain credibility by suggesting intellectual authority. The same is true in the twentieth century. For example, Alfredo Rocco, one of the leading intellectuals of Mussolini's corporatist movement, argued that thanks to capitalist concentration and mass production, society would be reshaped "according to the requirements of the great industrial empires and their structures."[23] Interestingly enough, that is exactly what Blair says has happened and it fits perfectly with the order of freedoms proposed by Bush and the Canadian government.

Rhetoric is formalized, received wisdom. But this desire to imitate intellectual authority also involves creating abstract notions that obscure real events. The Nazis were among the originators of this approach.[24] Particularly unpleasant tasks were given engineering or business descriptions. Abolishing political parties was called "putting into the same gear." Extermination camp victims were subjected to "special handling." We have continued with this mechanistic description of human events. Getting rid of employees is now called downsizing. The French call it *degraissage*—degreasing.

This type of abstraction is the natural outcome of a society broken down into interest groups. Indeed one of the difficulties faced by citizens today is making sense of what is presented as material for public debate, but is actually no more than the formalized propaganda of interest groups. It is very rare now in public debate to hear from someone who is not the official voice of an organization. How could these spokespeople possibly say anything that was not in the direct interests of their group? Even when we hear think tanks speaking out, we are not hearing thought. We are hearing rhetoric in defence of those who finance them.

As for pure propaganda, the selling device aimed directly at the public, it is essentially the same as advertising. Indeed we tend to forget that the methods of private advertising, like those of public propaganda, were developed as one in Germany and Italy during the 1930s and 1940s.

"The crowd doesn't have to know," Mussolini often said. "It must believe. . . . If only we can give them faith that mountains can be moved, they will accept the illusion that mountains are moveable, and thus an illusion may become reality." Always, he said, be "electric and explosive."[25] Belief over knowledge. Emotion over thought.

One of the characteristics of propaganda is that wherever possible, music and images replace words. This is particularly easy on television and in films where words are innately of tertiary importance next to the picture and the non-verbal sound.

We all know the uncontrollable, liberating or inspiring

effects music can have on us. As can images in a more direct way. These are effects that language can only very rarely accomplish. I am not suggesting some register of higher and lower arts, but different balances when it comes to separating out different functions.

Language is essential for rhetoric because the words and their structures are used to set out the false parameters. For propaganda, language is virtually irrelevant. That's the point of it. The real skills of the propagandists turn on the manipulation of music and image. These two arts may have difficulty formulating intellectual ideas, but they can quite naturally express the emotive. Love, religion, nationalism, patriotism can be celebrated. But they can also be manipulated to wipe out thought. There is nothing new about this. What is new is that the modern propagandists have become experts at using the images and non-linguistic sounds of modern communications technology to provoke feelings which stand in the way of self-examination.

The odd thing is that the tendencies of serious music—the art which in the past has produced the true magic of uncontrollable liberation—have turned in the second half of the twentieth century towards an arid, mechanistic rationalism. With a few remarkable exceptions, the field of public engagement in contemporary music has been left wide open to the propagandists.

What we now recognize as the two forces of political salesmanship and commercial advertising first coalesced in Leni Riefenstahl's film *The Triumph of the Will*. There she celebrated the 1934 Nuremberg rally of the National Socialist Party. Her use of the camera and the way she juxtaposed images with music removed even a hint of conscious meaning. People saw and believed. The selling of Coca-Cola or Calvin Klein underwear today is drawn directly from these methods, as is the staging of most contemporary political events. Many of you may react to this sort of argument by saying, but that is just advertising, as if to say, this is to be expected and can be ignored. That would unfortunately be naive. Advertising production costs are high multiples of those devoted to programming. The money used to produce a twenty-second spot for McDonald's would finance hours of television programming. In terms of straight expenses, the money paid for print news is a fraction of that paid for print advertising. Propaganda is therefore the purpose. Content is the frill or decoration.

None of this would matter were propaganda not the negation of language. It destroys memory and therefore removes any sense of reality.

I am loath to add to the negative view of television, but it does quite naturally fit the characteristics of advertising or propaganda. The stream of images and sounds overwhelms meaning. Serious programming exists, but it is not the natural product of the system.

In April 1995, President Clinton gave his fourth formal press conference—the first in eight months. Many people were shocked that only one of the three national networks carried it. The other two carried on with their sitcoms. This was an evolution from the days when everyone quite naturally stopped commercial broadcasting in order to communicate something thought to be in the shared public interest.

The virtual shutting out of President Clinton and his message was, in fact, part of a natural evolution. In a corporatist society, only self-interest and the specific matters. What's more, television is perhaps finding its real measure. A few months before the president's press conference, a study group asked American magazine editors to name the most remarkable events of the year. The O. J. Simpson trial was first. The hockey strike was third. A violent figure-skating quarrel was fifth. Again, many were shocked by this list of priorities. But was this not a natural expression of the Western country most dependent on propaganda—i.e., television? And is this sort of phenomenon not accentuated by the United States' having what is now the worst public education system in the Western world?

The existence of high-quality national public education school systems for the first dozen or so years of training is the key to a democracy where legitimacy lies with the citizen. At first hearing, this may sound like a motherhood statement. But the reality is that throughout the West—not just in the United States—we are slipping away from that simple principle of high-quality public education. And, in doing so, we are further undermining democracy.

Why is this happening? Theoretically because of money shortages. But there is no shortage of funds for those areas of higher education which attract the corporatist elites. Indeed, as money is siphoned off from the public-school level to the favoured areas of higher education, so the quality of public education drops and more parents opt for private schools. In removing their children they also remove any real commitment to the system and accentuate the shift. Of course, the taxation and administrative systems relating to the lower and higher levels are complex and technically separate. But from a distance what can be seen is nevertheless a shift of interest, commitment and funds.

There is no mystery surrounding the central role of public education. The revolutionary industrialist Robert Owen argued during the early Industrial Revolution in Britain that it was "the most powerful instrument of good that has ever yet been placed in the hands of man."[26] He also demonstrated at his model factory town of New Lanark that you could make high profits and finance education at the same time. Even Adam Smith believed that "the difference between the most dissimilar characters, between a philosopher and a common street porter, for example, seems to arise not so much from nature as from habit, custom and education."[27] Yet Smith's followers today are in the forefront of the movement to ease off the public commitment to basic education. The central theme today revolves around "quality," which actually means that the emphasis should go onto feeding the best up through the system to the elite structures. This is a standard hierarchical, corporatist approach.

Interestingly enough, the evidence indicates that producing the best educated elite in the world doesn't actually help a country. The two nations in the West most devoted to this approach—Britain and the United States—also have the most persistent and widespread social and economic problems.

To the extent that there is a new interest in public education, it is largely focused on aligning basic education with the needs of the job market. This apparently practical approach is illusory. Concentration on technology—computers for example—will simply produce obsolete graduates. The problem is not to teach skills in a galloping technology, but to teach students to think and to give them the tools of thought so that they can react to the myriad changes, including technological, that will inevitably face them over the next decades. What's more, this move to job alignment is led by the managerial class—public and private. But the crisis in our society and economy comes in good part from an oversupply of managers—dead weight being carried by the rest of the economy. These managers—the guardians of corporatism—give comfort to the higher levels of education as it continues to split knowledge into ever narrower specializations.

Those of us who believe in universities must not hold back from criticizing them out of fear of further weakening them in a time of crisis. That would be false friendship. The universities have become to a great extent the handmaidens of the corporatist system. This is not simply because of the academic specializations and their impenetrable academic dialects, which have become in turn the veils of governmental and industrial action.

A far worse criticism would be that of the betrayal by much of higher education of their wider mission. If the universities cannot teach the humanist tradition as a central part of their narrowest specializations, then they have indeed sunk back into the worst of medieval scholasticism. The need to rise above self-interest and the narrow view has always been a problem between writers and society. We can find Dante lecturing the elites of Florence for being "all too intent upon the acquisition of money."[28] Or Jonathan Swift mocking the academics for their obsession with abstract theories that ought to work. In the Academy of Laputa he visits bottlers of sunshine extracted from cucumbers, then goes into another chamber filled with a horrible stink. There he finds

the most ancient student of the academy. . . . His employment was an operation to reduce human excrement to its original food, by separating the several parts, removing the tincture which it receives from the gall, make the ordure exhale, and skimming off the saliva. He had a weekly allowance from the society of a vessel filled with human ordure about the bigness of a Bristol barrel.[29]

This brings to mind the work of the Chicago School of Economics on the natural balance of the market mechanism. Somehow, it just won't balance. However, they receive a somewhat larger allowance than a Bristol barrel of ordure and miraculously remain, if you will forgive a change of images, the vestal virgins of received wisdom.

The central problem here is a university community that does not teach the elites to rise above self-interest and the narrow view. It cannot because it has itself slipped into the self-interest and the narrow view that comes so easily in a world of professional corporations.

This is particularly a problem in the social sciences, which have contributed more than most to the rise of passivity. Why? Because they labour still under the burden of being false sciences. Their experiments do not provide any measurable progress in the manner of a real science. In place of real evidence they are obliged to pile up overwhelming weights of documentation relating to human action—none of which is proof, little of it even illustration. This sort of material carries the force of neither history nor creativity. What they are working with is circumstantial evidence. It is meant to create the impression of evidence by the force of weight. Whether this is credible or not, it becomes the basis of theoretically fixed measurements—a social truth has theoretically been established. This impression of knowledge leads to passivity in the social scientist. They claim to produce truths, but these are too fragile to produce anything other than passivity.

Political science is perhaps the greatest victim of this phenomenon, but it is the consequences of the 'truths' of economics that are the most important. "To be the slave of pedants," Mikhail Bakunin said, "what a fate for humanity."

Is this relentless drive for narrowness actually inevitable? Does our possession of ever-increasing particles of information require this fracturing approach to education? Does it work? Does it actually produce knowledge? Understanding? Or does this confinement of introspection produce what Kierkegaard called "contemptible rancour"?

The answer of the Enlightenment to the university schoolmen of their day was that their introspection wasn't working and change was necessary. Change meant a return to the humanist vision with greater openness to reality. The result was a leap in creativity, an enrichment of language and a spreading of knowledge.

Given that our approach resembles a return to the methods of the schoolmen, there is no need to be surprised at how smoothly the universities are fitting into the corporatist structure. Each profession has its box and each plays its circumscribed role. Already during the 1930s and 1940s, Germany and Italy suffered from this phenomenon. The majority of the academic leaders rushed forward to collaborate with the new, anti-democratic regimes, and began producing intellectual texts to beef up the official governmental corporatist ideas.

I'm not suggesting that our universities are today filled with Martin Heideggers in Nazi uniforms. What I am saying is that we are faced by a crisis in language and communication. This crisis is being accentuated, not eased, by the universities. We are faced by a crisis of conformity brought on by our corporatist structures. While the universities ought to be centres of active independent public criticism, they tend instead to sit prudently under the protective veils of their own corporations. We are faced by a crisis of memory, by the loss of our humanist foundation. The universities, which ought to embody humanism, are instead obsessed by aligning themselves with specific market forces and continuing their pursuit of specialist definitions, which are apparently their protection against superstition and prejudice. Yet, in a society of specialists, who deal with each other in their specific areas by duelling with references, definition becomes a means of control—a way to replace the search for understanding with an all-absorbing maze of road signs.

Peculiar marginal phenomena, such as political correctness, are usually presented as assaults on freedom of speech and academic freedom. It might be more accurate to describe them as just another aspect of the complex internal battles for control of the various academic corporations. Competing schools of rhetoric hide competing corporatist forces seeking power.

As for the alignment of education and market forces, of course in some circumstances it may actually be useful. But in general those circumstances involve trade school disciplines—such as the schools of business management—which don't belong in the university at all. They would be far more effective if they were funded and run directly by industry as independent apprenticeship institutes.

What the corporatist approach seems to miss is the simple, central role of higher education—to teach thought. A student who graduates with mechanistic skills and none of the habits of thought has not been educated. Such people will have difficulty playing their role as citizens. The weakening of the humanities in favour of profitable specialization undermines the universities' ability to teach thought.

Let me go back for a last time to Socrates' defence of the examined life. It was in the last real paragraph of his speech that the famous phrase came. I'll quote it in its proper context:

Perhaps someone may say, "But surely, Socrates, after you have left us you can spend the rest of your life quietly minding your own business." This is the hardest thing of all to make some of you understand. If I say . . . I cannot "mind my own business," you will not believe that I am serious. If on the other hand I tell you that to let no day pass without discussing goodness and all the other subjects about which you hear me talking and

that examining both myself and others is really the very
best thing a man can do and that life without this sort
of examination is not worth living, you will be even
less inclined to believe me. Nevertheless, gentlemen,
that is how it is.

To which I can only add that that is indeed how it is.

III

FROM CORPORATISM
TO DEMOCRACY

THE MOST POWERFUL FORCE possessed by the individual citizen is her own government. Or governments, because a multiplicity of levels means a multiplicity of strengths.

The individual has no other large organized mechanism that he can call his own. There are other mechanisms, but they reduce the citizen to the status of a subject. Government is the only organized mechanism that makes possible that level of shared disinterest known as the public good. Without this greater interest the individual is reduced to a lesser, narrower being limited to immediate needs. He will then be subject to other, larger forces, which will necessarily come forward to fill the void left by the withering of the public good. Those forces will fill it with some other directing interest that will serve their purposes, not the larger purposes of the citizen. It would be naive to blame them for occupying abandoned territory.

74

There are those who talk about individualism as if it were a replacement for government. There are others who see it as the enemy of government.

Let me begin from the self-evident. We are more than one. We are more than a family. We are more than several families. We are many tens of millions. We exist, therefore, in societies.

It has been several millennia since those of us in the West have been able to live outside society, except in odd, temporary cases. The opening of the American West, for example, was, for better or worse, a short-term exception available to a small number of people. In Canada the West was opened without the larger social structures falling away. There are a few people today who can live virtually alone in the Arctic on research stations and the like. They constitute a few hundred of us out of millions.

The individual therefore lives in society. That is the primary characteristic of individualism. The only question is what form that society will take. As I have already pointed out, the form of society turns upon where legitimacy lies. There are four options—a god, a king, groups or the individual citizenry acting as a whole.

How then could individuals possibly replace government? In a democracy they are government. This myth of the triumphant, unattached individual is pure romanticism and, I repeat, romanticism is a handmaiden of ideology.

Individuals do not beat large companies or defeat large armies. Why would one expect them to replace governments? The point is that there will be a government as there has always been. People ask: What kind of government? How much government? I think the primary question is:

Whose government? If individuals do not occupy their legitimate position, then it will be occupied by a god or a king or a coalition of interest groups. If citizens do not exercise the powers conferred by their legitimacy, others will do so.

Many of those who see individualism as an alternative also believe that government should be formally excluded from certain areas. Public enterprises are the first thing to go on their list for exclusion. Some wish to reduce government to the minimal occupation of dealing with violence—interior violence (law and criminality), and external violence (defence and foreign affairs).

The citizenry might well wonder why they should put artificial limits on their only force. The power we refuse ourselves goes somewhere else. Yet no other legitimacy is capable of disinterest. If the citizenry agree to exclude themselves from any given area, they are automatically excluding the possibility that in that domain the public good could have any role to play.

A moment ago, I referred to those who see government as the enemy of the individual. They believe that government has fallen into the hands of one of the other three legitimacies.

Many individuals in identifying government as their enemy have focused almost exclusively on the bureaucracy of government. Their belief is that the bureaucracy has taken over. This is a perfectly justifiable fear containing large elements of truth. But attacking the problem at that level—government is bureaucracy and bureaucracy is the enemy, therefore government is the enemy—is to miss the point and to invite far worse.

In fact, this bit of pure logic suffers from the classical fallacy of the undistributed middle. The logic involved is so flawed that, although it is in the style of the medieval schoolmen, it would have been rejected by them as an inferior specimen of abstract reasoning.

Nor is it particularly useful to worry about the theoretically dubious intentions of bureaucrats. Most of them see themselves as civil servants in the full sense of that term and are well intentioned. Nor is the problem that the public bureaucracy in particular has become so bloated as to be uncontrollable. The twentieth century has seen an explosion in all types of management. Our entire education system is aimed at creating managers of every sort. Managers of the government, yes, but business is also dominated by a top-heavy bureaucracy. I would suggest that today the problem of managerial dead weight is far greater in the private sector than in the public. I would suggest that one of the key reasons that the private sector has been unable to revive and reinvent itself over the last two decades has been a lack of creativity brought on by a managerial rather than a creative owner-based leadership. A second key reason is that the cost of the managerial superstructure is now far too heavy for the producing sub-structure. The managers are weighing the economy down.

It is therefore naive or disingenuous for those leading the fight against government to suggest that society will be reinvigorated by smaller government. Responsibility will simply have been transferred to an equally if not more sluggish bureaucracy in the private sector. What's more, by demonizing the public civil servant they are obscuring the matter of the citizen's legitimacy and of the public good which only that legitimacy can produce. People become so obsessed by hating government that they forget it is meant to be their government and is the only powerful public force they have purchase on.

This is what makes the neo-conservative and market-force arguments so disingenuous. Their remarkably success-ful demonization of the public sector has turned much of the citizenry against their own mechanism. Many of us have been enrolled in the cause of interests that have no particu-lar concern for the citizen's welfare. Our welfare. Instead, the citizen is reduced to the status of a subject at the foot of the throne of the marketplace.

A single line from David Hume lies at the heart of this argument: "Nothing is more certain than that men are, in a great measure, governed by interest."[1] The tendency has been both to drop that qualifying clause—"in great mea-sure"—and to use the remainder of the phrase out of context in order to suggest that the public good is a fiction and that self-interest must rule. Self-interest, it is suggested, is best served by the marketplace.

However, that isn't really what Hume said or meant. Yes, he was a bit sceptical about human qualities. And yes, he believed in "the civilizing powers of the commerce which was then transforming Western Europe."[2] But he also sought how civilization could best limit the negative effects of self-interest. As his biographer, Nicholas Phillipson, puts it:

All of Hume's philosophy, all of his history, was to be directed towards the goal of teaching men and women to seek happiness in the world of common life, not in the life hereafter, and to pay attention to their duties to their fellow citizens rather than to a superstitious god.[3]

God has been replaced today by another ideology called the marketplace. Hume may have admired commerce. He didn't see it as a deity.

But even if you do take the market theorists' interpretation of Hume at face value, why should that encourage the citizen to abandon government in favour of the private sector? After all, if man is governed by interest, then those who succeed have no obligation to worry about the 99 percent living at various levels below them.

Adam Smith was very clear about how the monied class—the masters, as he called them—act in their own interest if allowed to:

Masters are always and everywhere in a sort of tacit, but constant and uniform, combination, not to raise the wages of labour above their actual rate. To violate this combination is everywhere a most unpopular action, and a sort of reproach to a master among his neighbours and equals. We seldom, indeed, hear of this combination, because it is the usual, and one may say, the natural state of things. . . . Masters, too, sometimes enter into particular combinations to sink the wages of labour even below this rate. These are always conducted with the utmost silence and secrecy, till the moment of execution. . . .[4]

That was Adam Smith, I repeat, not Karl Marx.

The process Smith describes may sound familiar. The argument in favour of dropping wages today is that high salaries, given global competition, are self-destructive. Smith, however, attributed the masters' attitude to pure self-interest: "In reality high profits tend much more to raise the price of [a piece of] work than high wages."[5]

My point is that the individual and the government are linked together by an artery. If we act to sever that artery by replacing or opposing a central role for government, we cease to be individuals and revert to the status of subject. If democracy fails, then it is ultimately the citizen who has failed, not the politician. The politician can always find a new place in a new configuration of power—witness the growing attachment of the elected to private sector interests.

I would argue that to a great extent we are already well engaged in the act of cutting our own arteries—in both the wrists and the throat. If we are slipping into such a foolish act, it is largely because we have allowed ourselves to be convinced by our own elites that the democratic system is a secondary product of the free market system. And so, if the system and its managers—supported by their acolytes in departments of economics around the West and by the invasive buzz of their eager neo-conservative courtiers—if all of these people and institutions indicate that there must be changes, well, we bow our heads in respect.

Let me therefore lift my head long enough to expand a bit more on the true roots of democracy and individualism. I've spoken of both our humanist origins in Athens and the sources of freedom of speech. I've described bits of that twelfth-century renaissance which produced the modern intellectual liberation of the individual from the status of subject.

It was a process which affected many parts of society. For example, religion saw the rise of individual confession. During the preceding 1,000 years the confessing of sins had been done rarely and in general as a group absolution. Power lay with the priests as the essential intermediary between mankind and God. Suddenly, confession was something done and done frequently by the individual. It was recognized that not only do individuals sin, but he and she also have the right to individual forgiveness. Interestingly enough, the emphasis was not on priestly absolution but on an automatic absolution from God if the sinner had good intentions, which of course was between him and God. If the intentions of the believer were to be recognized as important, then the priest had lost a fundamental authority over what until then had been mere subjects.[6] This rise of the very idea of intent was central to the subsequent rise of individualism and democracy. Intent is a form of self-knowledge.

The same century saw the rise of personal portraits: that is, portraits no longer painted as stereotypes of the subject's social condition. Artists began signing their names. They were individuals, responsible for each visual act, not functionaries. Juries arose—thus citizens took responsibility for justice being done, and the weight of their votes counted. This was a major step away from direct democracy (i.e., mob justice) and from hierarchical or qualitative justice in which the power to decide lay with experts or those in authority.[7] In the villages, citizens chose their own local officials, made up their own regulations and administered them. In the towns, associations, unions, fraternities and guilds sprang up. As in the villages, members of these organizations were equal members. They voted and administered as equals.[8] These guilds were quite different from the hierarchical special interest groups that the corporatist movement sought to create in the nineteenth and early twentieth centuries and which have such power today.

These original guilds led to increased public services. Santa Maria della Scala—the hospital in the centre of Siena, in northern Italy—has been in service since the eleventh century. It was a creation of the public good involving various citizen groups.

John of Paris was writing a few years later that the "natural instincts" (*instinctus naturalis*) of individuals caused them to form communities which made up the state.[9]

In that same twelfth century, Aelred of Rievaulx was talking about the three loves—love of self, of others and of God. These three, "though obviously different, yet so amazingly dovetail into one another that not only is each found in all of them and all in each, but where you have one there you have all, and should one fail, all fail."[10] Note that these three loves have nothing to do with faith, hope and charity, the standard hierarchical qualities of a faithful believer as recognized by the church. Note also that faith and hope were passive qualities. The believer's faith and hope were expressions of what he would receive from divine forces. Charity also was passive for the vast majority who were rarely in a position to do more than receive the moral, ethical and concrete charity of the elites.

In this same era love poetry grew to celebrate the single male–female relationship. Satire—that basic tool of the individual citizen—was reborn.

Eventually the twelfth-century humanist renaissance of the individual faltered before the onslaught of a bureaucracy of Catholic lawyers who had begun to reorganize the papacy. Royal families began to grab away the power of their citizens in an attempt to centralize their kingdoms. A certain bitterness grew in humanist circles, particularly against the professional careerists—the specialist courtiers of the day.

Yet the humanist movement by no means died. In the thirteenth century the Magna Carta did far more than settle power on the barons. Particularly in clause 39, the rights of all free men were laid out. Essentially no free man was to be dealt with by authority outside the law. Over the years that term quickly expanded from "no free man" to "no man" (Edward III statutes, 1331) to "no man of whatever estate or condition" (1334).

Thomas Aquinas cleverly laid out the concept of the natural versus the supranatural; that is, the citizen versus the faithful Christian. The natural was regulated by the active Hellenistic virtues—Justice, Temperance, Prudence and Fortitude; the supranatural by the passive official Catholic virtues of faith, hope and charity. This meant that the individual citizen could now participate in public affairs without being overwhelmed by Christian requirements or assumptions.

A few years later Dante in *Monarchia* declared that "man alone was the constituent member of the human civilitas"

and Marsiglio of Padua that "acting in their totality as a community of citizens, [men] now possessed sovereignty, because
they alone were held to be the bearers of original power."[11]

This whole humanist movement fell back for a while,
then advanced again with the translations of the Bible in the
sixteenth century, which took powerful language out of the
hands of authority and put it into the hands of the individual. Part of that wave of humanism was led by Erasmus;
another part by the Italian Renaissance. The next setback
came with the Reformation and its reinforcement of authority. The result was the rise of pessimism or passivity because
of predestination. Almost at the same time, Loyola and the
Jesuits breathed fire into the Counter Reformation by adapt-
ing reason to their purposes—undermining humanism and
individualism.

But then the revolution in England in the middle of the
seventeenth century brought a whole new class to the fore as
Cromwell was supported neither by money nor the big families but by the yeomen and the gentry. The decline, later in
the century, of the whole idea of hell—with its threats of eternal fire—led to the rise of the idea that the majority had the
right to heaven. That, in turn, led to theories of democracy.

You will notice that through this whole process there has-
n't been a single mention of the role of economics, let alone
of the determining role of economics. That's because there
wasn't any. Any more than there was in the whole Enlightenment movement.

In general, democracy and individualism have advanced
in spite of and often against specific economic interest. Both
democracy and individualism have been based upon finan-

cial sacrifice, not gain. Even in Athens, a large part of the 7,000 citizens who participated regularly in assemblies were farmers who had to give up several days' work to go into town to talk and listen.

How is it then that we have fallen into taking seriously someone like the economist Milton Friedman who walks about equating, in a silly, indeed an immature manner, democracy with capitalism?

I suppose, in part, the answer is that that other view—the traditional anti-democratic view—has been slowly advancing behind a variety of masks for much of this century. Mussolini found his financing in the large industrial corporations by promising them that once in power he would discard democracy to make Italy flourish and government effective. Émile Durkheim, one of the founders of sociology, had already laid out the ideal structures of corporatism in which the state and the interest groups would be as one. "The corporation's rule secures for the state the deferential citizenry . . . and so frees it to govern on the basis of 'morality itself . . . not the deformation it undergoes in being incarnated in current practices which can express it only imperfectly' because they are 'reduced to the level of human mediocrity.'"[12] "Current practices" and "human mediocrity" are references to democracy.

The neo-conservative godfather, Michael Oakeshott, after showering contempt on democracy, decried ideology and reason in favour of common sense and practical experience. But when he addressed himself to economics, he was abruptly converted into what I can only call a rational ideologue who sees economics as a scientific abstraction completely independent from the realities of human society. Listen to him:

> Economics is not an attempt to generalize human desires or human behaviour, but to generalize the phenomena of price. And the more completely it leaves behind the specifically human world, the more completely it discards the vocabulary which suggests this world, the more unambiguously will it establish its scientific character.[13]

Thus, social order should be based upon human experience except, inexplicably, when economics are in question. Economics are to be treated as an absolute scientific truth.

Dozens of other corporatist and market theorists toiled away through the thirties, forties and fifties. Mihaïl Manoïlesco, Alfredo Rocco, Friedrich von Hayek. What linked them was a religious devotion to the market and an inability to see government as the justifiable force of the citizen. That is, their inability to see the human as anything more than interest driven made it impossible for them to imagine an actively organized pool of disinterest called the public good.

It is as if the Industrial Revolution had caused a severe mental trauma, one that still reaches out and extinguishes the memory of certain people. For them, modern history begins from a big explosion—the Industrial Revolution. This is a standard ideological approach—a star crosses the sky, a meteor explodes, and history begins anew.

The result is that you find well-known management

experts like Peter Drucker declaring today that "the nanny state is a total failure."[14]

Well, actually, it isn't. A great deal of what it does, it does very well. True, some serious problems have now developed, caused in part by management leadership and in part by too many incremental changes over too long a period. In addition, no one has experienced more than a partial nanny state. Let's not exaggerate reality.

But what is the meaning of wanting to demolish everything rather than considering repair or consolidation? The meaning is ideology. Those who have a miraculous vision of the world created in seven days or, in this case, from the Industrial Revolution on, require a total break in order to assert their model. And at the heart of this model, whether market-centred or corporatist, is the idea of interest and the denial of disinterest.

What I am describing is not a new problem. I've mentioned Dante, in the late thirteenth century, castigating the elites of Florence for being "all too intent upon the acquisition of money." In 1993 the retiring head of the French secret service (the DGSE) spoke to his assembled agents. He said the most dangerous situation they had to deal with was "the extraordinary rush for money in all its forms" and "the corruption of the elites." He said "the governing classes—political and economic—in much of the world, now treated money as if it had no odour," so that the clean is mixed with the criminal.[15] This surprisingly extreme statement from a public official—mind you, on his last day in the office—is nevertheless not a surprising description of a society that believes only in self-interest.

But while corporatism limits society to self-interest, it is far more than that. When I look back over the early and recent definitions of what corporatism was to be, I am continually amazed by how close we have come to those intentions.

First there is the continual confusing of industralization with capitalism with corporatism; the sort of confusion that ought to drive a modern economist crazy, but doesn't because all three fit together in a comfortable, flexible way. All three are interest oriented. They are now seen to be about organization and capital.

Remember: the origin of corporatism in the second half of the nineteenth century lay in two things—the rejection of citizen-based democracy and the desire to react in a stable way to the Industrial Revolution. These original motives would evolve into the desire for a stable managerial, hierarchical society.

Listen to Émile Durkheim again. The corporations are to become the "elementary division of the state, the fundamental political unit." They will "efface the distinction between public and private, dissect the democratic citizenry into discrete functional groupings which are no longer capable of joint political action." Through the corporations, "scientific rationality [will] achieve its rightful standing as the creator of collective reality."[16]

It all sounds like obscure nonsense. But think about our society. How are real decisions made today? Through negotiations between the specialized and interest groups. These are the fundamental political units. Citizens who rise, citizens who win responsibility, who succeed, enter into these units. What about the distinction between public and private? The concept of arm's length is evaporating. Government services are slipping into private hands. And the government is adopting private industry standards and methods. As for the individual, the one-third to one-half of the population who are part of the managerial elite are indeed castrated as citizens because their professions, their employment contracts and the general atmosphere of corporate loyalty make it impossible for them to participate in the public place.

Now listen to the first three aims of the corporatist movement in Germany, Italy and France during the 1920s. These were developed by the people who went on to become part of the Fascist experience:

1. shift power directly to economic and social interest groups;
2. push entrepreneurial initiative in areas normally reserved for public bodies;
3. obliterate the boundaries between public and private interest—that is, challenge the idea of the public interest.[17]

This sounds like the official program of most contemporary Western governments.

Finally, there is Philippe Schmitter, who in 1974 published a paper called "Still the Century of Corporatism?"[18] This sparked the creation of a whole industry of academics working on what they called "neo-corporatism." Together, they began the process of legitimizing a corporatism that had been intellectually unacceptable since 1945.

The words "interest representation" are central to Schmitter's theory. He writes with an assumption of "the erosion/collapse of liberal democracy."

Schmitter and the others seemed to assume that this new corporatism would involve a deal between the government and the private sector. They saw it as perhaps resembling what the English tried to do in the 1970s, when the unions, business and government sat down to thrash things out. Or, with deep misunderstanding or misrepresentation, these apologists mentioned Sweden, where this was done much more successfully. What they didn't see was the growing isolation of the steadily fracturing specialist and interest groups and the opening of borders that would make corporatism an international affair in which the governments and the employees were increasingly weak players.

The peculiar thing is that this little army of academics around the world is constantly debating the merits of 'state' corporatism, which they see as a dictatorship, versus 'society' corporatism, which they praise as merely removing some of the citizens' democratic powers. They never seem to discuss whether it is a good thing for the citizens and democracy to be losing *any* power. Or whether democracy has *enough* power.

What is remarkable about corporatism is its inherent strength. What we are witnessing today is its third or fourth run at power in a little over a century. Each time, it is beaten back—as it was during World War Two—then, a few years later, it reappears, redesigned and stronger.

Even the model of the strong corporatist chief reappears in a new guise. Look at the Italian neo-fascist leader Gianfranco Fini, who is now a key government player. He makes a point of resembling a well-dressed merchant banker. Look at the Austrian neo-fascist leader Jörg Haider, who now wins a quarter of the votes in national elections. He resembles a movie star and has literally designed his aura in movie star manner. This, of course, is only a detail in the latest rise of corporatism. After all, the system is the same throughout the West, where, in most places, perfectly normal party politicians are holding power.

However, the great unspoken issue is why no Western population has been asked to choose corporatism, let alone has demanded it. It simply creeps up on us, a bit more every day.

Bismarck played the corporatist card very hard when he was German chancellor in the second half of the nineteenth century, continually holding it out as a threat to the democratically elected members of the Reichstag. He even let it be known, through others, that he might go as far as a *coup d'é-tat*[19] in order to change the system. The atmosphere which he left certainly weakened the Reichstag, both then and after World War One.

It could be argued that we are now in the midst of a *coup d'état* in slow motion. Democracy is weakening; few people would disagree. Corporatism is strengthening; you only have to look around you. Yet none of us has chosen this route for our society, in spite of which our elites quite happily continue down it.

Mussolini said that "liberty was all right for cavemen, but civilization meant a progressive diminution in personal freedoms."[20] He had a kind of *idiot savant* feeling for the twentieth century at its worst.

Certainly corporatism is creating a conformist society. It is a modern form of feudalism with none of the advantages of the early urban guild system, where obligation, responsibility and standards played a role. It's not surprising that Japan, Korea and Singapore should do so well in such an atmosphere. They resemble the perfect corporatist state or benign dictatorship.

As for us, we are reverting back to our role as the faithful servant of the church. We continue to struggle with the old question—which has been with us since Gregory the Great in the sixth century—of whether to obey a superior even when the order is unjust.

The slow emergence of strict modern corporatism can be seen in our attempts, over the last half-century, to deal with this issue of obedience. It was given enormous play after World War Two when German officers and officials were tried and convicted at Nuremberg for having obeyed orders. Today we are inundated by trials and official inquiries revolving around this same question of whether or not to obey orders. What if contaminated blood is being used in the health-care system? What if a car or a plane has a faulty part?

We are—almost all of us—employees in some sort of corporation, public or private. Increasingly, those who follow orders are being acquitted. Why? Because increasingly our society does not see social obligation as the primary obligation of the individual. The primary obligation is loyalty to the corporation. It is, as Jung described it, "that gentle and painless slipping back into the kingdom of childhood, into the paradise of parental care." Why? Because "all mass movements slip with the greatest ease down an inclined plane made up of large numbers. Where the many are, there is security; what the many believe must of course be true."[21]

We usually think of mass society in Marxist terms or in those of modern communication technology. But nothing could be more of a controlled mass than a corporatist society. Max Weber, the other founder with Durkheim of modern corporatism and sociology, predicted the emergence of a world of efficient, exact managers, all of them trained to solve problems.

Of course, there has always been another view. Flaubert wrote of the "mania for conclusions" as "one of humanity's most useless and sterile drives."[22] He saw this—now one of the manager's most desirable attributes—as a minor expression of religion. Those who have the truth must have the answer.

We are faced by this truth every day. We hear nuclear experts, for example, blaming the problems of their industry on "extreme environmentalist groups," playing "cleverly on the factors of 'dread' and 'the unknown' in the public mind."[23] It is here assumed that the public couldn't know enough to understand and it isn't worth wasting much effort explaining things to them.

Mexico has acquired a whole new layer of these managers over the past few years—almost all of them educated in the United States. Called *los perfumados*—the perfumed boys—they have been in charge of the country's radical modernization program. When the peso and the economy collapsed at the end of 1994, the new managers were at least partly to blame. But the attitude of the corporatists was one of line loyalty. The United States Under-Secretary of Commerce for

Trade, Jeffrey Garten, went public in order to say that he had full confidence in them (the United States was paying the bill for the crisis). He said Mexico's U.S.-educated technocrats were "one of the very important links that exists between the United States and economic teams in virtually all Latin American countries. Under no circumstances can that be anything but a great advantage."[24]

Now that is almost word for word what Field Marshall Sir William Robertson, the British Chief of the Imperial Staff, said about Allied staff officers at the end of World War One. Most soldiers and field officers thought them responsible for a prolonged slaughter and guilty of the worst incompetence.

None of what I am describing is a simple matter of Left versus Right. Corporatism cuts across political lines. The official voices of reform are as much a part of the structure as are the voices of the Right. Look, for example, at the American liberal attempt to put in place a decent health-care structure. First, an American president was elected by the people with, as his principal platform, health-care reform. Once in power he turned to the relevant elites and they produced a new health-care structure which was a technocrat's nightmare. Even its supporters couldn't understand it. The president put this proposal forward for debate and it was flung aside with the flick of a wrist.

How? Why? In large part because the whole approach to reform had been so corporatist, so technocratic, so complex, that most people—even allies—could not get involved in the debate.

But at the end of the day the question was far bigger. An

American president was elected to do something. He was prevented from doing it, not by Congress, but by the corporatist structure. Can we say that such a country is functioning as a democracy?

One of the ways of dealing with that question is to look at the effect of corporatism on the elected representatives of the people.

The corporatist idea that elected representatives are merely representing interests has led them to apply pressure directly on the politicians. The result has been a remarkable growth in the lobbying industry, which has as its sole purpose the conversion of elected representatives and senior civil servants to the particular interest of the lobbyist. That is, lobbyists are in the business of corrupting the people's representatives and servants away from the public good.

This may be done over the long term or the short term, with cash in bank accounts or on country weekends, with understandings about jobs or board positions to be made available on retirement. Once the principle of legalized corruption had been accepted, the methods of corruption turned out to be inexhaustible, as the leadership of the previous Canadian government demonstrated. This year, Conservative MPs in London are furious because they may have to declare what they earn as "parliamentary consultants." They may even be banned from continuing as paid agents for lobbying firms. But Britain seems no worse than anywhere else.

Those governments freshly elected elsewhere on "clean the house out" platforms frequently turn out to have been on the take before their arrival, if we are to judge the new governing parties in Italy and the new Gaullist government in France.

The point of these examples is not to demonstrate that politicians are corrupt. It is to suggest that the discomfort in our system comes largely from a long-term undermining of the representative system by the corporatist system. Those who are elected know that power has slipped elsewhere. Their frustration, to put it in the most general terms, leads them to try to get something else of the situation. They are being corrupted in a much more profound sense than the merely financial.

Cromwell said that "the King's head was not taken off because he was King, nor the Lords laid aside because Lords . . . but because they did not perform their trust." Instead they formed an alliance with a group of big London capitalists, who loaned money in return for titles and privileges.[25]

Virtually every politician portrayed in film or on television over the last decade has been venal, corrupt, opportunistic, cynical, if not worse. Whether these dramatized images are accurate or exaggerated matters little. The corporatist system wins either way: directly through corruption and indirectly through the damage done to the citizen's respect for the representative system.

Yet in no Western parliament has more than marginal action been taken to deal with this problem. From within the system it seems as if nothing more than the details of corruption can be dealt with—registrations, open accounting and so on. But from the outside the entire system is seen as intolerable and the population is losing confidence while it waits for a fundamental change. The same could be said for the vast majority of those elected. They gain no pleasure from this degrading system and most are as honest as the average citizen. But the system seems unable to free itself from the tentacles of what corporatists such as Schmitter admiringly called "interest representation."

In spite of this, governments continue to deliver services that are and have been historically better in the long run than those provided by the private sector. Our lives are filled with these services. They run so smoothly that we scarcely notice them.

Yet in imitation of the marketplace, government is busily transforming itself to meet business standards. It isn't quite clear what these are when it comes to public service. The flaw in the logic can be seen in very simple things: for example, there is a tendency now to refer to the citizen as a customer of the government. The customer of the police. The customer of the fireman or the health officer. But we are not customers. We haven't walked into a shop to think about buying. We are not going to make a purchase and then walk away. We are not even customers with long-term (in business this is rarely very long) service contracts. We are the owners of the services in question. Our relationship is not tied to purchase or to value for money, but to responsibility. Not only are we not the customers of public servants, we are in fact their employers. I suppose that if this mania for business terms is uncontrollable, then the most accurate term to describe the citizen would be shareholder. But even that is inexact because (1) we cannot buy and sell our shares (we are stuck with them for life) and (2) we do not own these shares for profit.

This little linguistic slippage within the bureaucracy shows how essentially directionless the corporatist system is. Once the idea of management for management's sake takes over, the organization, whatever it is, begins to skitter about aimlessly, following one expert system after another, obsessed by problem solving without really considering the problem in its own terms. And control. Everything is a matter of control. Yet control, like efficiency, is a secondary or tertiary business, well behind policy and purpose and, for that matter, effectiveness.

As Léon Courville, the president of the Banque Nationale du Canada, has said, the manager's principal aim is to remove uncertainty, thus forgetting that uncertainty is essential to successful action.[26] A terrible fear of error possesses them, because in a pyramidal structure there is no admission of the possibility of error. Management is about systems and quantification, not about policy and people.

Robert McNamara, near the beginning of a long tome designed to deal with his blunders in Vietnam, nevertheless pauses to talk about quantification as a revelation. "To this day, I see quantification as a language to add precision to reasoning about the world."[27] Given his record on the counting of body bags, among other statistics, I should have thought he might have considered softening the sentence. But then an obsession with quantification does tend to end up in superstition.

In spite of his track record of errors, McNamara remains in many ways the star of the systems men. At the height of the Vietnam War he gave a speech that set out what the system and some of those in it believe:

Undermanagement [of society is] the real threat to democracy. . . . To undermanage reality [is to let] greed . . . aggressiveness . . . hatred . . . ignorance . . . inertia . . . [or] anything other than reason [shape reality]. If it is not reason that rules man, then man falls short of his potential.[28]

The key word here is "rules." Man *must* be ruled. This is the Hobbesian, corporatist view. If not kept under control, man and woman will run amok. Some time later McNamara moved on from the Pentagon to apply his same system to the World Bank. There he played a major role in creating the Third World debt crisis. Years before he had said, "Running the Department of Defense is not different from running the Ford Motor Company or the Catholic Church, for that matter."[29] Now that is a very fine summary of the structure that underlies corporatism. His career is eloquent proof that what he says is not true.

Still, there is no point in demonizing McNamara. He is merely an unfortunate, large catastrophe in an unfortunate, much larger system. Even his idol, John Kennedy, believed strongly in the management approach and used all the new methods. For example, he avoided calling cabinet meetings. Though cabinet members represented a formal element in the democratic system—a table of counsellors approved by the mechanisms laid out in the constitution—he preferred to see them separately in order to control the agenda and to spend the rest of his time with his courtiers. The bloated White Houses of Ronald Reagan and George Bush—with 1,300 courtiers—were direct descendants of Kennedy's Camelot.

There is nothing new about bureaucracies—as opposed to management. Since the Roman Empire they have tended to grow uncontrollably and to lose purpose. This is not evil. It's just a characteristic.

What is new is the devotion of the whole elite to the bureaucratic ethic—that is, to management—as if it were a primary skill. This is the product of corporatism. It is what happens when you rank reason and method over content.

The result is that those elites which should counterbalance the bureaucracy, do not. Instead, time is wasted on fights between the interest groups: public versus private; regional versus national; national versus international; all blaming each other for whatever it is they say is wrong. Whatever they claim, these fights are rarely over policy. Corporatism is about interests and the division of those interests. Their fights are over who gets what.

In this context there is no disinterest and no direction and no reward for thought or disinterested participation. The result is a growth within the population of contempt for the elites. What follows from that is what we are now experiencing: the rise of false populism, which is usually linked to the enemies of democracy.

I'd like to pause here, just for a moment, on the subject of reason, which lies at the heart of democracy's problems and, indeed, of management's. First, I am not attacking reason *per se*. I am attacking the dominance of reason. Reason as an ideology. Sensibly integrated along with our other qualities, reason is invaluable. Put out on its own as a flagship for society and for all of our actions it quickly becomes irrational.

We all know that reason came into the modern world with a fanfare of great expectations. It came to save us from arbitrary power and religious superstition. As early as the thirteenth century, Thomas Aquinas was saying that "every man must act in consonance with reason." And that great idealist, Robert Owen, in the midst of the Industrial Revolution, was certain that "man has no other means of discovering what is false, except by his faculty of reason."[30]

The difficulty is that, from Plato's *Republic* on, reason and utopia have been inextricably linked. This has been more than a marriage of convenience. It is reason that is used to explain why each successive utopia—I should say ideology—is inevitable. And it is reason that, we are told, will make it run. The truth about how we should be organized will thus be revealed. It isn't surprising that the ideologies of the past two centuries have claimed to be the children of reason.

Many people have attacked this presumption, but they themselves have tended to do it from an ideological point of view. The Frankfurt School made brilliant critiques that were undermined by their own Marxism. "The new order of fascism," Max Horkheimer wrote, "is reason revealing itself as unreason." Michael Oakeshott attempted to do the same from the Right, but was undermined by his pretence of shuffling conservatism. Bertolt Brecht found himself under attack in East Germany for his opera *The Trial of Lucullus*. He was accused of "a relapse into doubt and weakness."[31] Reason knows no doubt. It is strong because it finds the answers.

Most of the Communist parties are now gone. What

remains in the West, and in the old Communist bloc wherever anarchy doesn't reign, are the structures of corporatism. In particular, the technocrats have inherited the Platonic marriage of reason and ideology. That's why they react somewhat hysterically when arguments are raised against the clear leadership of reason. They say they fear the opening of the door to superstition. To our dark side. In reality they fear losing their own self-confidence or being faced with a trial in which the successes and failures of reason are compared.

This desperate need for reason and the accompanying latent addiction to solutions are good examples of the unconscious at work. Take McNamara during the 1960s on his new nuclear strategy—flexible response: ". . . basic military strategy in general nuclear war should be approached in much the same way that more conventional military operations have been regarded in the past."[32] This is a perfectly rational statement that suggests lunacy. He might have found it helpful, even calming, to read a bit of Diderot before announcing his latest truths. The following is Diderot's definition of facts—those elements so beloved in the creation of rational truth—as laid out in the original *Encyclopédie*:

> Facts: You can divide facts into three types: divine, natural and man made. The first belong to theology, the second to philosophy and the others to actual history. All three are open to question.

The problem, as you can see, is not reason, but what we

have done to reason by raising it to a state of divinity. Various professors in our schools of philosophy have tried to deal with this problem by developing a sub-category of reason: instrumental reason. This term is intended to describe reason as it is actually applied in the real world. But such a distinction only accentuates the problem. It is as if they were saying, now we have both the deity and the deity's representative on earth. Reason as a deity is an untouchable perfection. Instrumental reason—the representative on earth, so to speak—is responsible for everything that goes wrong, but might go right. Such an approach takes us right back to earlier demeaning distinctions. For example, there was that of the untouchable divine monarch versus his incompetent, corrupt ministers. Or just as once the flaws of the Christian faith—the Inquisition, for example—could not be addressed because burning several thousand people was on a lower level than the Holy Trinity, so now the follies of reason—the nuclear strategy of flexible response, for example—cannot be addressed because it is merely instrumental reason.

This is perhaps an expected development in a corporatist society where the large picture, the longer term, is lost in the incremental details of specialization and fact collecting and reason is raised even higher to the status of a father figure. Or rather a God the Father figure. That this problem of specialization and fact collecting stretches deep into our universities, even into our departments of philosophy where the larger picture, the longer view would be particularly valuable, only makes the arrival of small-picture experts more expected.

I said earlier that one of corporatism's problems—apart

from being anti-democratic—is its aimlessness. That comes in part from this myriad of small-picture experts. A world in which those trained to know are not permitted to look up and look around. This is knowledge reduced to ignorance. The more knowledge is limited to a single corner, the more ignorant the expert. John Ruskin said technocrats were an "intricate bestiality." Perhaps, but it isn't really their fault. This is what our society requires of them.

An interesting example of the small picture versus the big is the matter of cuts in public programming. The desperate need to cut the fat in order to get at the various government deficits has been high fashion for several years now. Governments keep cutting, public service programs get thinner, the citizen gets less for the tax dollar, yet the deficits don't go away and the cry for more cuts grows louder.

Now the curious thing is that the people who have led the campaign for public cuts are the senior management in the private sector. Their voices are amplified by the think tanks which they finance, as well as by various economists and their friends in the press. What this group has rarely mentioned is that the large private corporations have also been engaged in a fat-cutting program. Their bureaucracies had also got out of control. They were far too deeply in debt. In fact the fashion for cutting in the private sector started a good fifteen years ago and the results have been in for some time. In general, what they call "downsizing" has not worked. In companies like IBM, Sears and GM, tens of thousands of workers were laid off. It did not produce a turnaround. Not in the first year and not in the second, when thousands more were laid off. In fact, many companies sickened. Some died. Yet it had all been done with the best intentions.

The problem they have discovered is that "you can't shrink to greatness," as the president of Petro-Canada put it.[33] When you cut seriously, the first thing to go is creativity and risk taking. The company slips into an encircled mentality. Employee morale plummets and so does productivity. The advisers then call for more cuts to get the company out of its slump. The general term for this state is corporate anorexia.

Industry-wide results of such severe self-inflicted punishment between 1989 and 1994 were as follows. Only 34 percent of companies showed an increase in productivity. Only half showed any increase in profits. Employee morale dropped by 86 percent.[34]

The problem is that cuts can't produce growth or prosperity or effectiveness, but cutting—a negative tool—is the natural implement of a corporatist society.

If the religion is self-interest, then no one is paid or encouraged to take the distance that disinterest requires. And only with a certain distance can you identify fundamental problems. Just as the characteristics of religion pass from one ideology to another, so too the superstitious belief that suffering is necessary to pay for our sins has been passed on and reformulated as the cutting process.

The curious thing in all of this is that private-sector leaders, knowing that they themselves were caught up in corporate anorexia, still pushed the public sector to go down the same route. But this cannot have been malevolence on their part because they are honourable men, all honourable men. At worst it was perhaps malevolent mediocrity. Somehow, no one was able to look up from the little picture and see the relationship between these two machete-armed patrols.

Indeed, the experience of the public process of cutting has run exactly parallel to the private. The more they cut, the more the citizenry are annoyed because they are paying the same taxes and not receiving adequate services. They then blame the public sector for ineffectiveness and either go along with or call for more cuts.

Had the private-sector leaders been malevolent—which surely they were not—in their call for public cuts, then it would have been a very effective way to undermine support for public services. Here perhaps is a good example of how the failure of an elite to lead effectively drives them further into the arms of ideology where everything is inevitable. The suffering of the public sector certainly provides some twisted comfort to those who came to grief in the private.

Clearly, what is needed is not cutting, but the consolidation of years of incremental growth in services. This ability to stop periodically, re-examine and consolidate progress is easy if people are able to deal with problems in a calm way through an overview. The corporatist atmosphere makes this almost impossible.

Yet consider our society. Everywhere in the public domain there has been a good half-century of rapid growth. Most of that was incremental. Perhaps the single most important innovation needed today is a calm look at the overall effects of what we have accomplished, followed by serious attempts at positive consolidation. We must force ourselves out of the corporatist obsession with form in order to concentrate on the content that is at stake.

Instead we are falling prey to an anti-public sector campaign that has created a sense of panicked urgency around
the subject of privatization and cuts. We have slipped into
the religious flagellatory mode of asset-stripping the citizens' public possessions. Considering how much effort
went into building this society, we have nevertheless
engaged in an unconscious process which can best be
described as slow, masochistic suicide. And suicide, except
in very rare cases, is the product of an inability to see ourselves in the context of our reality. Death appears to be the
door of salvation from our illusions.

What was it Socrates said to the jury after they had condemned him to death?

"But I suggest, gentlemen, that the difficulty is not so
much to escape death; the real difficulty is to escape from
doing wrong." Wrong, he said, "is much more fleet of
foot."[35]

The escape from doing wrong is where I would like to end
this discussion of public life, by glancing at some areas in
which we are not yet identifying the effort needed to escape.

Decentralization of bureaucratic power is increasingly a
popular theme. The hated massive bureaucracies will have
the important public-service programs taken out of their
hands. These will be broken up and moved down to regional
and local levels where the citizenry can have a human relationship with more modest groupings of bureaucrats and
even have an impact on the nature of the programs.

This could make good sense if two conditions were met:
funding guarantees and national, indeed multinational,

standards. Countries inside the European Union have more or less dealt with this. The rest of us, in a fit of childlike unconsciousness, can't seem to draw the elements together. It isn't all that difficult. Central governments everywhere are in a long-term funding crisis, in good part because they get less and less tax revenue from the large corporations who, in a global marketplace, play one country off against another. Who can blame them if we are too incompetent to organize ourselves at a multi-government level? Instead, our governments are handing essential, but now unfundable, programs down to the regional level in the name of increased democracy. But the regional governments are also in a funding crisis and in a far weaker position *vis-à-vis* the large private corporations. "Too bad," say the central governments. "You'll just have to raise taxes to pay for the programs. Go on, assume responsibility!"

Whenever governments adopt a moral tone—as opposed to an ethical one—you know something is wrong. Of course, the regional governments can't raise taxes. The source of revenue would simply leave for another region. In fact, the effect of decentralization without guaranteed funding and national or multinational standards is a competition between regions for the lowest possible tax rates. The regions with the fewest tax sources must drop to the lowest tax rates. The standards of programming drop with the taxes. Inequality between regions reappears rapidly, to such an extent that the programs may not even survive.

So the point of decentralization is not really to deal with the tension between big government and the citizen, because there are actually three players in this triangle: the citizen, big government and big business. Any move by two players is affected by the third. Interestingly enough, the big companies are mostly in favour of decentralization. The president of a large Canadian bank recently broke Adam Smith's "utmost silence" of the employers and said publicly that national standards in social programs were nonsense. Everyone, he said, has different needs. He didn't, unfortunately, go on to explain the different regional needs of cancer and heart attack victims.

Interestingly enough, those who are against government social programming are almost all in favour of decentralization—the neo-conservatives, the market economists, the funded think tanks. As Captain Joshua Slocum, who in the nineteenth century was the first to sail solo around the world, put it: "Fishes will always follow a foul ship."[36] More precisely, William Kristol, an important neo-conservative lobbyist in Washington, says: "Send [all the social programs] down to the state [level], let the states experiment much more, and have private charities take care of people."[37]

More or less the same grouping is in favour of referenda and "direct democracy" as against the slow tedious grind of representative democracy. The false simplicities introduced by referenda and direct democracy are much more open to the effects of Heroic leadership—that is to say, manipulation. The Heroic leader's direct relationship with the people is combined with an attack on what Jörg Haider, the highly successful Austrian neo-fascist leader, called "party politics." Cabinet debate is "idle gossip and a waste of time,"[38] as is parliament. That is the central theme of Silvio Berlusconi's politics. He alone, via his dominant ownership of Italy's television networks, will have intercourse with the people. Sylvester Stallone, in his role as the justice giver, Judge Dredd, clarifies the situation: "[It's] almost fascism, it's almost a military state, but that's the price of having someone protect you."[39]

The key to the referendum society is that it turns on a mystic evocation of past grievances, gathered together into a churning, aggravated spleen, where they are magnified and isolated from reality. Everything that is not a grievance disappears. This anger is then dovetailed into an heroic solution. Simple, absolute, salvatory. An answer.

The modern referendum, as Napoleon understood when he invented it, is the ideal consummation of the rational as irrational, of the anti-democratic posing as democracy. The complex issues of reality, which democracy can deal with in its own slow, indirect way, are swept aside by single, clear issues, often modelled on single human qualities—either we must have common sense, or we must have reason, or we must have memory. It is as if any combining of human qualities is impossible.

Not surprisingly, both the referendum and direct democracy are a happy marriage with corporatism. The complex, real questions are dealt with behind the scenes through efficient "interest mediation" between the different interest groups. As for the citizenry, they are occupied and distracted by the fireworks of their direct involvement on the big questions and their direct relationship with the big people. A simple "yes" or a "no" and history, they are told, will be changed, as if by the wave of a magic wand.

Henry Kissinger used to talk of historic destinies being changeable only in moments of white heat. He claimed to have taken the idea from Metternich. In fact, Mussolini said it best: "Only blood . . . makes the wheels of history turn."[40] Referenda and direct democracy provide the sensation of blood without the reality; what George Grant called "decisiveness . . . at the expense of 'thoughtfulness.' "[41]

Alvin Toffler and his wife—and apparently their disciple, Newt Gingrich—seem to have understood all of this, consciously or unconsciously. A pamphlet written by the Tofflers and introduced by Gingrich adds the Dada of technology to the Napoleonic methods of manipulation through referenda and direct democracy. The message in their pamphlet, *Creating a New Civilization*,[42] is that technology makes not only possible but inevitable—that old ideological characteristic—government by semi-direct democracy and referenda.

Majorities will soon be looked upon, the Tofflers claim, as "an archaic ritual engaged in by communicational primitives." They propose an "heretical" leap forward into "minority power." The suggestion is that we, the alienated citizens, are the minorities. In reality they are proposing: (1) a return to the medieval system of qualitative in place of quantitative majorities; that is, a hierarchical society; and (2) the legitimization of the corporatist system, of rule by interest groups.

Technology, the Tofflers say, makes traditional democracy archaic. They wrongly describe this technology as the third great wave of societal change. More accurately, it is the Nth important wave of technical change since democratic principles were first established 2,500 years ago.

Finally, the Tofflers insist that "the institutions of government must correlate with the structure of the economy and the information system. . . ."

A more sensible approach might be that technologies come and go. Economic structures evolve and change. Society adjusts. But democratic basics persist in spite of the Tofflers, Gingrich and the chorus of corporate voices.

"Must correlate"? Did you notice? They insisted that we must correlate with economics and technology.

"Necessity," William Pitt said two centuries ago, "is the plea for every infringement of human freedom. It is the argument of tyrants; it is the creed of slaves."[43]

What the corporatist system is telling us in various ways is that the democratic system is no longer appropriate. This attitude involves the active or passive agreement of large parts of our elites.

But democracy is not what they imply. It is not about prosperity. You can have poor democracies. And you can have prosperous dictatorships. The world today is peppered with authoritarian market-based societies where Adidas, fine cooking, sexual pleasure and higher education prosper. Nor is democracy merely necessary as a protection for the poor. Even basic authoritarian societies need some sort of social contract, unless they are ready to make constant use of brute force.

Democracy is simply about the nature of legitimacy and whether the repository of that legitimacy—the citizens—are able to exercise the power its possession imposes upon them. We are having great difficulty today exercising the power of legitimacy. It has therefore shifted away into other hands.

In the final chapter I'll come back to the practicalities of individualism and democracy. But the problem we face is not one of incomprehensible complexity. Unlike the tormented unconscious acts with which Freud dealt and that respond only marginally to self-knowledge, societies can quite easily use consciousness to provoke action. Nothing in our current crisis is untouchable because of great mystic forces of inevitability. Technology and the market are useful phenomena to be respected. But they are neither gods nor wild animals. Legitimacy itself is not a matter of mystics but of practicality, as are the actions of a healthy democracy.

IV

FROM MANAGERS AND SPECULATORS TO GROWTH

DID THE INDUSTRIAL REVOLUTION bring us prosperity?

If we begin with such a basic question, it may force the arid and convoluted world of economics into some contact with the reality it is intended to explain.

Well of course it did. The prosperity and comfort the West has experienced over the past 70 years would not have been possible without the Industrial Revolution.

But that is the answer to another question. Certainly, without the technology of early, modern and late capitalism, we could not have created and sustained this culture. And it was by no means just a matter of technology. Capitalism itself helped make this possible. And the free market. And a growing capital market to finance investments. And trade, because galloping trade was a major factor, on an increasingly global scale. So without technology, capitalism, the free market, the money markets, free trade and globalization—concepts still at the very centre of our lives—we could not have financed and maintained our standard of living.

That's all very well, but let's go back to the question— Was it the Industrial Revolution, composed of these factors, that raised our standard of living and brought us an historically unprecedented level of widespread prosperity?

Certainly it brought prosperity to a new class of owners and managers, but they represented until half a century ago only a tiny percentage of the population. In Britain, in the late eighteenth and early nineteenth centuries, most of the population left a simple rural or an artisan existence to move into the turbulent world of factories. In the earliest days of the Industrial Revolution, the children of the poorest had tended to start as workers at the age of fourteen. They and the adults worked a twelve-hour day, including time for meals and rest. Traditional holidays remained in place from the pre-industrial period. However, a few decades later, in the early nineteenth century, it was common for children to begin as workers at seven or eight years old and to work fourteen hours a day in the unhealthful and dangerous factories. Many of the traditional holidays were simply ignored by the companies. It was a question of work or be fired. And in spite of working so much harder and longer, the labourer was worse off than a quarter-century earlier.[1]

This experience very much parallels that of many in the developing world today. For example, the experience of the millions who left simple but stable rural lives for the slums of Lagos is virtually identical to that of the nineteenth-century British farmer become worker.

But surely what I'm describing were temporary conditions, the unfortunate, inevitable disorder of revolutionary change? The standard market forces view can best be expressed in a mess of metaphors: Eggs had to be broken while the 'invisible' hand of the market mechanism reached down to rebalance the social structure in the context of new economic conditions.

Well, actually these conditions could not be called temporary. They persisted until the second half of the nineteenth century and then only began to ease gradually. There wasn't any serious spreading of prosperity throughout the population until the twentieth century. In many ways things got far worse for a very long time. For example, the development of the mechanized cotton mills created much of the market for slaves to pick American cotton. Slavery had always existed, and in almost every civilization around the world. But it had been a piecemeal business, usually the result of individuals, Europeans or others, being captured in war or convicted in the law courts. The sugar and cotton field slaves represented a major revolution—the enslaving of a race purely for economic reasons. To put it crudely, the standard of living of the individual, reduced to slavery, dropped.

The long-term pattern of the Industrial Revolution was to institute a lower financial standard of living and declining conditions of life. The result was a full century of unimpeded social decline and disorder. At life expectancy levels then common, this represented many generations; a long-term pattern, not a temporary adjustment. What's more, during this long, unimpeded run, the economic forces were even unable to establish a stable imbalance. The market simply repeated, repeatedly and mechanically, the cycle of slow build to a boom followed by a bust. The market did not and does not learn because, being devoid of disinterest, it has no memory. There can be no such thing as a natural market equilibrium.

Well, if the Industrial Revolution—with all its qualities of technology, capitalism, the free market, the money markets, free trade and globalization—brought unstable but long-term poverty, what brought prosperity? Quite simply, as the nineteenth century advanced into the twentieth, a growing number of citizens publicly opposed the conditions created by the Industrial Revolution. They exercised the power of their legitimacy—which included demanding a widening of that circle of power until it included all adults, through universal suffrage, achieved only after World War One.

The public demands for change came in many forms. Sometimes the need for reform was expressed from above, sometimes it showed itself as blind fury in the street. The process gave birth to everything from Marxism and fascism to liberalism, socialism and reform conservatism. Most of the reforms that brought prosperity were the result not of self-interested action but of disinterested action—citizens committing themselves beyond their personal interest in order to widen the public good.

There is absolutely no indication that the Industrial Revolution imbalance had a self-rectifying mechanism to achieve any social balance—by which I mean reasonably shared prosperity. It was the citizenry and democracy that forced the economic mechanism into a socially acceptable and reasonably stable shape; what I would call the shape of a civilization.

I am not suggesting that this slide down into despair and then up into prosperity happened in a clearly sequential manner. There was the continually intersecting confusion of political cycles, war cycles and the various economic cycles. As recently as the end of World War One a strange euphoria set in. The citizenry relaxed its guard, perhaps in relief after the lunacy of organized, rational, military butchery. What seemed to be a period of unstoppable market-led prosperity set in.

The November 1929 issue of *McCall's Magazine* celebrated this victory with a conversation between novelist Sinclair Lewis, columnist Walter Lippmann and Will Durant, the popular historian of philosophy. The atmosphere in this conversation was summarized by the editor in his introduction:

Our prosperity is doubtless very great. Invention, machinery, labor-economizing devices, keep develop-ing so vigorously that, despite those who believe the machines will soon overwhelm and enslave us, both our output and our leisure time keep increasing. The worker, the artisan, as well as the housewife in the kitchen, have more leisure today than was dreamed of a generation ago.[2]

By the time the magazine actually reached the stands, businessmen were throwing themselves out of windows and the latest depression had begun. After that it seemed as

if we had finally learned our lesson: learned that the marketplace could not learn its lesson. Therefore it was up to the
individual as citizen, through a careful definition and imple-
mentation of the public good, to make sure that the innate
economic imbalance benefited from the rules of civilization.
Yet, here we are, a mere 65 years later, with a financial
market which by comparison makes that of 1929 seem
responsible, a stock market which, once again, moves in a
manner unrelated to investment in real production, declining real wages for the vast majority of the population,
chronic unemployment not as serious as that of 1929 but far
higher than statistics admit and high enough to stultify the
economy. Finally, real growth disappeared two decades ago
and has yet to return.

Even more astounding, we keep on hoping that we will
rediscover prosperity through this mechanism called market
forces. In imitation of the nineteenth century and the 1920s,
we are deregulating everything in sight and even restructur-
ing government and education along industry lines. We
have fallen back in love with an old ideology that has never
paid off in the past.

Now, there are those who will mistake what I say for an
anti-market tirade. They will be wrong. I love the market. I
like trade, money markets, global economic patterns, all of
it. It's like a game. It's fun for those who can afford to have
a sense of humour. But I'm not fool enough to mistake
these necessary and important narrow mechanisms for a
broad, solid, conscious force that can lead society. The history of the marketplace has been repeatedly written by its

actions. To ignore that history is to withdraw into severe unconsciousness.

The important conundrum for us is to understand how we have come to so forget our own history that we are now compliantly acting in a suicidal manner, believing that economics can lead—where in the past it has always failed to do so.

This is the question I want to illustrate in this chapter, with a few indications of how some simple public policy discipline might help us reassert our sense of belonging to a civilization rather than to an imaginary economic dialectic with inevitable conclusions.

Let me put it another way. If we did indeed defeat corporatism in the last world war and Marxism less than a decade ago, why do we cling to the basic corporatist belief in group legitimacy and the basic Marxist belief in economic determinism? I've said elsewhere, at least half seriously, that the only true Marxists functioning today teach in the Chicago School of Economics and manage our large corporations. I could add that these same people are the true descendants of Benito Mussolini.

But let's return to the question. Why are we unable to focus consciously on our own history? Why is the largest and best-educated elite in that history so insistent on handing the power—which we won and entrusted to them— over to an abstract, self-destructive ideology?

One possibility is that we are blocked by a combination of technocratic management and technocratic speculation. The technocratic management, produced mainly by business schools and departments of economics, is most comfortable functioning in large management structures.

Today the most obvious vessel in which to release their desires is the transnational or the very large national corporation. Their training and these structures have very little to do with capitalism or risk. They are reincarnations of the seventeenth-century royal monopolies. They are, if you like, a modern version of mercantilism. All statistics show that these big joint stock companies, managed rather than owned in any meaningful way, are poor long-term investors and poor investors in research and development. Creativity frightens the administrative mind and so they have a negative influence on innovation. And because they respond to the abstract theories of employment, they are poor job creators.

As for the speculative money markets, we are distracted from their innate rationality by the disorder they create. Reason here lies in the methods and skills of application. From the technocrat's point of view, the disorder of the speculative markets is the problem of others. From within they see the purest application of abstract theory, extremely complex, requiring specialist skills. Best of all, they see a world separated from any hint of reality. The finest technical minds seemed to be attracted precisely by this separation from the real. Even public officials are seduced by the intricate interior logic represented by the burgeoning financial speculative markets.

Our belief in salvation through the market is very much in the utopian tradition. The economists and managers are the servants of god. Like the medieval scholastics, their only job is to uncover the divine plan. They could never create or stop it. At most they might aspire to small alterations.

So they have power without responsibility; like the armies of *condottieri* who roamed Italy during the Renaissance; like the courtiers close to a king.

Now, power without responsibility is a basic form of illiteracy or ignorance. One of the characteristics of late scholasticism was that it prevented enquiry—that is, it prevented thought. The world was reduced to detailed linear argument based upon a fixed world view.

Educated, intelligent people thus slipped into a world of romance. The romance of what might happen, of what should happen, when at last the proper conditions were assembled—for example—for the Trinity to reign eternally or, today, for the market to balance. In such a world there is no possible reasonable opposition. Opponents are Girondins, Mensheviks, wet, naive, out of step with the truth. Those with power are passively certain of themselves as they wait to benefit from the inevitable.

Like other ideologues in power they become increasingly comic. Their language becomes parodic, even nonsensical. They will say that the nation is experiencing strong, real growth, and then, in the same paragraph, add that the nation is bankrupt. Well, which is it? It is common today to run growth and bankruptcy together the way medieval Catholicism—through the Inquisition—would say God is strong, good and kind, therefore we must torture you.

And those who oppose the policies of these passive technocrats tend to fall into the same parodic obsession with detail—for example, to develop a complex, conspiratorial view of the banks or the transnationals. But there is no need for a conspiracy. These are structures managed by servants.

Their logic is public and self-evident. Complex, long-range conspiracies require conscious leaders. To treat the technocrats as such is to give credence to their illusions about themselves.

A more realistic approach to our economic problems would be to focus on the repeatedly negative, self-flagellating, doing-harm-to-do-good characteristics of the managerial class. I mentioned in an earlier chapter their literally Old Testament approach to public debt. The sin. The terrible shame of having sinned against the god of prudence. The need to atone. To suffer for having had it too easy. All of this nonsense has drawn attention away from the "historically high levels of private sector debt," to quote the discreet annual report of the Bank for International Settlements.[3] The private-sector managerial class is in a guilt war with the public-sector managerial class. And the private sector, although it has been far less competent in its spending, particularly in an income versus indebtment comparison, has won the war. That public debts are a recurring problem which can be dealt with in many ways, all of them non-Biblical, has been lost to us in the hysteria that has led to binges of program cutting.

I talked in the previous chapter about the self-flagellation of heavy cuts and of how they rarely pay off. They leave a depressed, brutalized victim, hardly a candidate for growth and effectiveness.

Debts and cuts are just two of what I call the little ideologies, the miniature ideologies, that distract the managerial class from any admission of their fundamental passivity before the inevitable. Efficiency is another one to watch for.

This minor shop floor characteristic has been promoted to near membership in the Holy Trinity. Notice that it is efficiency we always hear about, not effectiveness. Effectiveness is about content and policy delivery. Efficiency is just an abstract and primarily negative term.

All the things which technocrats fear are incapable of efficiency—risk, thought, doubt, admission of error, research and development, long-term investment, commitment to concrete places. Even identification with real production is inefficient because it does not conform rigorously to models. An obsession with efficiency prevents growth and stymies capitalism. For technocrats, one of the attractions of what is called the service industries is the servile and non-concrete character of such businesses.

What are we to make of these managers, who have had almost absolute control of Western business for some 30 years, the last 22 of which have been marred by general crisis? Did they play a role in bringing on the economic blockage? They certainly have failed to produce an economic recovery. I would say this is largely because the administrator's fear of uncertainty makes him exactly the wrong person for a crisis. Yet the business schools keep expanding. They are the profit centres of most universities, which shows how far the universities have strayed from their mission.

Stalin was perhaps the first structure man to demonstrate that the best way to power was through the control of personnel. It permits you to promote allies and minions without reference to real accomplishments. No matter how badly the MBAs are doing, they just go on hiring clones of themselves.

Léon Courville puts it this way:

Management, a science? Of course not, it's just a waste-paper basket full of recipes which provided the dish of the day during a few years of plenty and economic growth. Now the recipes are inappropriate and the companies which persist in following them will disappear.[4]

He is even more sceptical about public-school systems teaching management methods, which the corporate managers are pushing them to do. Just as the managers have pushed onto governments an obsession with cutting, years after the same policy failed in the private sector, so they are pushing onto the citizens' schools the teaching of a management methodology which, at best, was marginal to basic education but now is known to have been an outright failure.

At the centre of these miscues is a profound misunderstanding. Most business leaders who preach the ideology of capitalism, free markets, personal initiative and risk are themselves not capitalists. They are managers: bureaucratic employees specialized in methodology. They are men of reason. A capitalist has more use for other human qualities—common sense, intuition, creativity. The most interesting capitalists may even have memory. At the top of their bureaucratic business profession, the managers take fewer personal risks than a senior civil servant, who does not have the protection of stock options and golden parachutes.

Not only do the large enterprises the managers run not have a close relationship with the shareholders, many of them have large blocks of their shares owned by pension funds and their equivalents. These enormous funds are themselves administered by the same sort of managers.

And so they advance, hand in hand, down the road of false capitalism.

This is a domain in which the levels of self-deception are both high and rewarded. The manager has taken on the cloak of capitalism. He lectures the government on risk and incentive, but also pays himself as if he were an owner. The only shares he owns are received as part of a special financial arrangement with the company. Although Western economies have been stalled, along with general wage levels, the manager's income continues to increase. In a good year, some top American technocrats now get between $50 million and $100 million. In other countries it is only one to two million—amounts most real owners of smaller companies would be thrilled to earn.

It follows from all of this that the manager has had to replace an owner's talents with an alternate form of action in order to simulate capitalist activity. Mergers, acquisitions, deacquisitions and takeover battles have become their preferred tools.

If you cannot create, then buy a company that can. In particular, the large corporations buy small, personally owned companies that have made breakthroughs in particular areas. They are buying creativity, though once integrated into an administrative atmosphere that new rush of creativity soon slows and dies away. It is sucked out of them.

But the worst thing about this pattern is that the technocratic companies can afford to pay and over-pay for these injections of fresh blood. In the process of doing so they have bid up the market value of companies to the point where it is hard for the owners of small operations not to sell out. The result has been an expanding, abortive effect on economic development. Too often companies that would have consolidated their breakthroughs and produced a new generation of independent corporate leaders are being bought up and sucked dry in order to give life support to the rather ineffective larger units.

The merger and acquisition mania goes far beyond buying creativity. It comes in waves of managerial fashion intended to give the impression of action and policy. The 1980s were notorious for these frenzies of forced partner-changing. The year 1995 saw a growth in demergers. By halfway through the year in Europe there had been 31 major untyings of the knot worth $1.3 billion. Globalization makes it even easier to play this merger, demerger, merger game with someone else on a world-wide board. Everyone is kept busy. The money markets, instead of being used to finance growth, are more than happy to finance marital chair switching because the units bought and sold can be assigned a value. Investing in real growth would be far riskier because it would involve pushing forward into the unknown. That the constant exchanging of units means both artificially bidding up their value and indebting them is not the managers' problem. They are not owners. That they are generating a serious form of inflation is also not their problem.

Another aspect of this appetite for false corporate expansion has been the growing push from the private-sector managerial class for the privatization or selling off of public companies. Nationalization and privatization are mechanisms that periodically can be useful. However, an unnecessary move in either direction merely makes money for the political friends of the party in power. It is they, inevitably, who handle the sale and so earn large fees as lawyers, accountants and brokers. One way or another some of that money finds its way back to the political parties and/or their senior organizers.

What matter, some of you may think, so long as these services are released from the heavy hand of government and put into the competitive marketplace. Perhaps. But few of these state corporations were providing ineffectual services before being sold off. Otherwise no one would have wanted to buy them. Indeed, it is the services that don't work that are not being sold by governments. And I personally have seen no emerging pattern which indicates, either in studies or in public reactions, that once privatized the already adequate services have improved.

There is a more important factor directly related to the problem of technocracy. The privatization theory is that the economy is being held down by too much government involvement. Sell the public companies and so invigorate the economy. However, an economy has many parts to it. There is the solid, conservative side that provides goods and services. But, by its very nature, it cannot provide much leadership towards new growth activity. Then there is the riskier, faster moving side, where new investment, new ideas, new energetic leaders combine to build the future economy. One day they will be on the conservative side, but not for the moment.

Most of the government-owned industries belong on the conservative side, either by the very nature of what they produce—essential services like electricity or water—or because decades have already been spent fully developing the capacities of that domain. So the effect of the privatization movement is to take perfectly good private-sector risk capital and invest it in the non-risk side of the economy.

Most people vaguely feel that economies are without limitations; that people will invest where they wish and each sector will develop for the best. The reality is that economic activity is limited by the time and efforts the business elite can devote to it. The size of those elites, the financing available to them, the structures they work in, their mental and physical energies are all perfectly natural limitations on their actions.

There is an old management rule that one man can't administer more than twelve people. That number—twelve—has many mystical, pre-Christian roots, but the unconscious origin in this case is probably Christ and his disciples. As the New Testament explains, even the son of God couldn't manage twelve. Eleven was his maximum and the one-too-many brought down his whole enterprise.

So here we are, loading up the established part of the private sector with billions of dollars worth of solid, gilt-edged production and service units. Private industry energy and money that ought to be going into front-line capitalist activity is being diverted to the rear guard of basic production and services.

How could widespread privatization have any other effect than to slow down the economy? Look at Britain where the experience is most complete. Has the British economy taken off? Is it leading the way? Is its growth above Western averages? Has the debt shrunk? No. Aside from the speculative isolation ward of the City of London, the British economy is one of the most sluggish in the West.

There is a sidebar to privatization that illustrates the problem. The managers of these sold-off public services have rapidly bought into the illusion of the private-sector technocrats that they are capitalists. In Britain in particular the old water works and power boards soon found their bosses handing themselves enormous pay raises and generous stock options. These reflected no measurable increase in the quantity or quality of the services sold to the public, and therefore no improvement in the position of the shareholder's investment.

The general point here is that these large, lethargic public enterprises are ideal organizations for business managers who fear the unknown. With minimal risk, they can strut about in capitalist garb and lecture the public from the podium of private ownership.

Allow me a last example of natural management tendencies: the commercial property market. The explanation of the popularity of property speculation among the lenders—the banks and pension funds—is that they can measure property values. The ability of a loan officer to enter almost guaranteed values into his books makes property far more attractive than investment in risk venture capitalism. The guarantees attached to property values are largely an illusion, however, as we discover every decade or so when the property market crashes. The employee-lender doesn't really mind. He has had years without uncertainty. By the time the crash comes he may have been promoted or entered retirement. He has lived the illusion of value, with everything calculated and on paper. This is Robert McNamara's romance of quantification.

In any case, what really matters is what attracts the investor—not the lender—to the property business. It is not the values but the rental income. This is the kind of administrative, non-capitalist, non-capital good venture the managerial class loves.

Adam Smith described the phenomenon very clearly: "As soon as the land of any country has all become private property, the landlords, like all other men, love to reap where they never sowed, and demand a rent even for its natural produce." "Wherever capital predominates, industry prevails; wherever revenue, idleness."[5]

Today's managers are not even landlords. However, investment in property is one of their solutions to a profound desire for idleness. The result in our economies over the past few decades has been an unprecedented concentration on the construction of office buildings to house the growing managerial class. Headquarters. Regional headquarters. Local headquarters. Buildings are a concrete proof of the value of the manager. Offices must be filled because they represent functions. And so royal palace after royal palace has gone up. Skyscrapers containing more square metres of floor space than Versailles or the Imperial City in Peking. These are the earthly paradise of courtiers and of those who seek power without responsibility.

Property, privatization, mergers and acquisitions—these are only three of the manager's non-capitalistic diversions. There are dozens of others and each one of them can be given the legitimacy of a miniature ideology. What is the utility of this long critique of the managerial approach? Well, any number of perhaps helpful conclusions might be drawn. First, that we have lost all sense of Adam Smith's concept of "useful labour" and that the economists, business schools and private-sector management are responsible for that confusion. And that economics must be rescued from the dead end of econometrics and reintegrated into an approach that includes politics, history and philosophy. That business schools represent a serious failure and are an impediment to prosperity and growth throughout the West. They should be removed from universities and converted into an element—just one of the elements—of a business-financed apprenticeship system.

If obsessional behaviour on the subject of privatization is a corporatist diversionary tactic that slows growth, the citizenry must learn to identify it as such. After all, this phenomenon is particularly easy to analyse. And only then can it be resisted as an ideological insistence upon necessity. Instead of accepting constant fulmination about ownership, risk and productivity, when much of business leadership is actually engaged in management, card shuffling (mergers and acquisitions) and revenue seeking, the citizen and the share owner must learn to differentiate. Then they can decide which they want or what mixture of the two.

Is all of this unrealistic? Yes it is, so long as we continue to pump fresh prisoners of the management approach out of our universities and so long as public regulation facilitates, even encourages, false capitalism.

What I want to concentrate on for the rest of this chapter is the role that four economic pillars play in accentuating or reducing our unconscious, troubled state. What are these four pillars? Current received wisdom has it that they are the marketplace, technology, globalization and the money markets.

The marketplace has been constantly evoked over the last quarter-century as the source of freedom and democracy as well as the only possible force to lead us back to growth. But after two decades of having their way, the exponents of this theory have no results to show us. Like medieval inquisitors, they concentrate on any remaining details that may prove the devil's continuing presence. But they have been in charge, they have held and continue to hold the levers of power, and they have not produced. This is a very long trial period—five times the length of a world war, double the reign of Napoleon who changed the face of Europe, longer than the reign of Stalin or Roosevelt, whose regimes had such fundamental impacts.

Ideologues hold out the guarantee of divine knowledge and the promise of the kingdom to come. But "how dangerous a thing it is," Cromwell said, "to appeal to God the righteous judge." "You have appealed to the judgement of heaven. The Lord has declared against you."[6]

This experiment in market leadership has not reinforced democracy or individualism, nor has it brought growth. It has reinforced corporatism and it is therefore not surprising that the most effective corporatist states—Japan, Korea and Singapore, for example—have benefited most. Certainly, the rule of the market has produced no growth in citizen-based democracy.

When I was in Seoul a few months ago, the police emptied the apartment buildings in a sector of the city and sent in several hundred riot police to arrest a single worker who had made a pro-union speech in his unorganized factory. They broke down the door to his apartment, fired in tear gas and captured him *in flagrante delicto*, eating his breakfast. He was manacled and carried off to jail.

We often talk of the corporatist market system in Japan today but forget that the rise to power of the Japanese military in the 1930s was the direct result of an experiment with market leadership from the late nineteenth century on.

The founder of the modern currency futures market, Les Melamed, says that "the market place is the most democratic forum ever invented,"[7] yet there is no historical indication that this has ever been the case. During the Reformation there were ample opportunities to stand up for freedom and for various types of citizens' rights and individualism in the face of authority. The successful capitalists, however, kept their heads down and only chose their side once the battle was over.[8] The American revolutionaries—mainly gentry, artisans and farmers—had a similar experience. Most of the monied interests, particularly in New York, either remained discreet or quietly supported whoever was occupying the town at that time.

The contradictions in this claim that the market gave birth to democracy can all be found in that well-known economic theorist, Professor Jeffrey Sachs, who a few years ago advised Mikhail Gorbachev into economic disaster. Professor Sachs now runs around central Europe preaching the virtues of the marketplace-democracy marriage. Yet he also advises governments that their real model should be Asian; that is, corporatist and anti-democratic. "You're competing with Thailand and Malaysia," he said recently in Prague. If central Europe "behaves itself, [it] can grow at 5 percent a year until the end of the decade."[9]

Our essential difficulty is that we are seeking in a mechanism, which is necessary, qualities it simply does not possess. The market does not lead, balance or encourage democracy. However, properly regulated it is the most effective way to conduct business.

It cannot give leadership even on straight economic issues. The world-wide depletion of fish stocks is a recent example. The number of fish caught between 1950 and 1989 multiplied by five. The fishing fleet went from 585,000 boats in 1970 to 1.2 million in 1990 and on to 3.5 million today.[10] No one thought about the long- or even medium-term maintenance of stocks; not the fishermen, not the boat builders, not the fish wholesalers who found new uses for their product, including fertilizer and chicken feed; not the financiers. It wasn't their job. Their job was to worry about their own interests.

Why then did government fail to impose suitable long-term regulations? In large part because we do live in a corporatist society, where the public good is minimized and governments through their managers are expected to concentrate on "interest mediation," as the neo-corporatists put it. There is no room for thought at any level because there is no room for disinterest. A severe crisis seems to be required to shake up governments and remind them of their responsibility to lead. Only in these crises do the corporatist groups lie low and allow the governments to do their proper job.

The problem of industrial pollution is very much the same. As Robert Heilbroner put it in the 1992 Massey Lectures:

> Steel producers have no incentive to cut down on pollution, insofar as they do not pay the laundry or health bills to which it gives rise. As a result the market mechanism does not accurately serve one of the purposes that it purports to fulfill—namely, presenting society with an accurate assessment of the relative costs of producing things.[11]

In other words, the marketplace is capable only of calculating exclusive costs; that is, excluding all possible costs that interfere with profit. Leadership of society requires the calculation of inclusive costs.

To invoke the marketplace, as if calling upon the Holy Spirit, is to limit ourselves to the narrow and short-term interests of exclusion.

Our tone becomes even more reverential when we turn to the second pillar, technology. Yet technology is no more capable of giving leadership than the market. If the technocratic class so often invokes technology, it is because these inanimate objects can take on a trajectory of their own and so cover for the manager's inability to give leadership. The corporations can, however, through copyright, own these mechanisms and so receive revenue from them. This is why the large corporations have led an obsessional drive over the last few years to strengthen international copyright laws.

I thought of this, the essential modern worship of technology, when the other day I walked past the cast iron, green-painted, art nouveau public toilet in the gardens of the Champs Elysées. It was there that Marcel Proust's narrator brought his grandmother on each of their outings. Inside this tiny pavilion, a woman cleaned and took tips from users. She held court there, refusing insalubrious users, no matter how desperate their need of her facilities. She was known as *la Marquise*. The grandmother eventually had a stroke in one of the toilets.

Curiosity and need drew me in. It was still a public toilet with high standards. The inside, however, had been modernized so that the three toilets and the two urinals were controlled by turnstiles for which special tokens were necessary. The problem was that the new control system technology took up one-half the space and the useful objects—the real content—the urinals and toilets—one-third. You had to get through the turnstile and, if the first urinal was in use, squeeze between the barrier wall and the man relieving himself to get to the second, and do so without pushing the poor man into his urinal. It wasn't self-evident. Had I found the second urinal in use, I'd have had the same problem getting out of the system. Proust's grandmother would probably have had her stroke much sooner if she'd had to deal with the new technology designed to facilitate her movements.

Of course a great deal of technology does facilitate our actions. But it is rarely about more than form. Its effects on content are indirect, which explains the modern manager's great interest in systems technology. Take Microsoft's new operating system, Windows 95; consider the money spent on its launch; the atmosphere of consequential happenings; the articles written on its merits or lack of them. Listen to some of the new qualities, even new powers, conferred upon us by the use of this technology. The following is their description, not mine:

Windows 95 "gives you a place to throw stuff away." "[It] and you find the easiest way yet to open an application, get help or find a file you're looking for." "You can do things like call files anything you want. . . ."

These minor bureaucratic breakthroughs are in fact, if you exclude the use of less labour, a major backward step in their own terms when compared with Max Weber's technocratic ideal early in this century. What the machinery does is limit even our basic actions to its own level of ability.

One last quote:

"Start understanding—A faster way to get help, called the 'Answer Wizard,' lets you ask questions in your own words. Ask, 'how do I print a page sideways.'"[12]

What an interesting way to use the word "understanding." Is that what it means? Something related not to thought but to minor technical manipulations?

Communications technology is being introduced into schools at approximately this level. Essentially, a new, high-level course in typing is being presented as if it were fundamental education. Basic technical training is, of course, useful. But to treat it as anything more than that is to lock students into technology that will be obsolete by the time they graduate. The time wasted will also deprive them of the basic training in knowledge and thinking that might help them adjust to the constant changes outside.

An increasing number of schools are spending large parts of their budgets on computers and computer programs. Once in possession of enough equipment they can line up a classroom full of students behind machines where they can be educated in isolation by something less intelligent than a human. This sacrifices one of the primary purposes of education, particularly in a democracy—to show individuals how they can function *together* in society.

You will note that I am not in any way suggesting we don't need this technology or that it can't be helpful. But it is merely machinery and as such may be helpful or destructive depending on the direction we give it. For example, go back to the beginning of the modern technological revolution. Robert Owen, one of the most successful factory owners of the early nineteenth century, was convinced that the development of machinery would lead eventually to a world dominated by justice, equality and ethics. What's more, the efficiency of the machines would release humans from all but a few hours of daily labour.[13] Instead, the market has used this efficiency to eliminate jobs and, over the last decade, to begin driving wages and employment conditions back down again. It is thus returning to the model Owen believed would be a short-term phenomenon limited to the early stages of technology. "Since the general introduction of inanimate mechanisms into British manufactories, man, with few exceptions, has been treated as a secondary and inferior machine."[14]

This was exactly the system put in place through Taylorism at the beginning of the twentieth century. Frederick Taylor's "scientific management" saw men and women as mechanisms to be managed along with machines. This was at the heart of the teaching he built into the Harvard Business School. Taylor's assumption still lies at the base of most twentieth-century business school training.

Has the new communications technology changed all of this? Clearly Microsoft doesn't think so, if we are to go by their explanations of Windows 95. Clearly the market doesn't think so or it would have used technological efficiency to reduce work hours rather than to reduce workers, thus pushing the problem of unemployment onto the government which it is, at the same time, trying to strip down to minimums.

Do the new communications technologies offer an opportunity for change? Well, when the printing press was introduced, the result was not an economic revolution, but a humanist revolution, driven by language, beliefs and a desire to understand—the world was profoundly changed. But from its beginnings, the printing press was independent of governmental and business interests. That was its power.

High-technology communications have been quite different from their beginnings. Government and industry have been at the centre of development, constantly striving for control. Even as the information highway takes form, the public and private interests are carving it up as an information control system and a sales mechanism. Can the technology free itself? Technology doesn't seek freedom. Can those who use it, use it as the writers, printers and readers of books once used the printing press? Perhaps, though the possibilities are by no means clear at this stage.

I say this because the sheer size of the transnational groupings, both inside and outside the communications sector, leaves very little room for the independent player. I have already talked about the division of language into the irrelevant public level versus the relevant corporatist tools of rhetoric, propaganda and dialects. One of the results of the corporatist domination is that we are inundated by non-information information. Already government departments and corporations are beginning to flood the Internet with their rhetoric and propaganda, all in the name of public debate.

The third economic pillar is globalization. It is here that Adam Smith's "invisible hand" of the marketplace is most often evoked. But when you look at what he actually said, most of his concrete references were to local markets. Just one example: "If in the same neighbourhood, there was any employment evidently either more or less advantageous than the rest . . .",[15] then a suitable average wage would emerge. Smith saw the self-balancing market in a simple and limited circumstance where the options would be obvious to everyone. A small city in early industrial England, for example, might have four small factories, in the same business installed on the four sides of the same square. The owners could see each other across the square from their office windows. They lived on the same street. And the workers' lives were as one when they came out of the work rooms at the end of the day onto that small square. In such circumstances it would be possible to arrive rapidly at an equilibrium.

Smith may or may not have been right about that, but what he was describing was an entirely different situation from a global marketplace in which there are no limits. There can be no pendulum swinging, then settling into place, without a centre and fixed outer limits.

This is why, for example, we have seen a continual growth in global trade every year for years now, and yet this has not translated into increased prosperity for individuals. We are told that increased trade levels will bring growth back to life. But trade is already at historic highs and is having no effect on any of the key sectors.

A few decades ago we were told that only if inflation were defeated would growth revive. Subsequently we were told that the key to growth was to cut the fat in business. Then it turned out that the problem was the fat in government. Then salvation was to come through an increase in trade. We have done all of these things. Nothing has happened. Trade, like any other economic mechanism, can be extremely helpful in the right circumstance. It cannot in and of itself solve societal problems.

What's more, this isn't our first infatuation with trade. An examination of the second half of the nineteenth century shows that the results of the free trade movement were very mixed. Germany drew back in disorder. Japan, as I mentioned, ended in military dictatorship. Even Britain, the apostle of the movement, found its economy grinding ever slower as the century went on.

But trade is only one aspect of globalization, which of all the economic changes surrounding us is the one most insistently presented as inevitable and uncontrollable. When anyone protests about the effects of this evolution on jobs or living standards it's as if the Queen of Heaven in Homer's *Iliad* had spoken up in reply: "Dread Son of Cronos, you amaze me! Are you proposing to reprieve a mortal man, whose doom has long been settled, from the pain of death?"[16] With globalization we are deep within the will of more than the gods. This is pure Destiny, the most acute form of ideology. It doesn't matter what the effects are. Destiny must reveal itself.

The Singaporeans are involved in a remarkable experiment. They are developing industrial parks on Batam Island—a nearby Indonesian territory. The first park will employ 50,000 workers. Singapore's problem is that it has become the perfect miniature corporatist—that is, managerial—market civilization. Almost no democracy, little freedom of speech, the discouragement of individualism, but a high standard of education, living and therefore of wages.

They are therefore creating a tariff-free, cheap-production, industrial haven on Batam Island. It's just off their shores. Foreign companies will ask the Singaporeans to organize and build them factories. On a two-year contractual basis Indonesians will be produced to do the work at $260 per month per worker, all costs included. There will be no need for social infrastructure, no long-term commitments to workers, no unions of course.

In other words, they will have created a production system inside globalization but outside any form of civilization. A sort of limbo, devoted solely to production; a lunar landscape devoid of the characteristics of human society. This model is already being extended to operations in China.

Such tariff-free industrial zones are only the latest of the phenomena that bring pressure on Western governments and employees to limit their demands on transnationals.

Perhaps the key effect of globalization has been to force governments to shift the tax burden from large corporations onto the middle class. When the income tax rates can go no higher, this shift is continued through taxes on goods and services. Interestingly enough, exactly the same policy was followed by the Holy Roman Emperor Charles V in the sixteenth century. The result was that growth stalled, in spite of the gold and silver coming in from the colonies in Latin America. Think of that traffic in gold and silver as the equivalent of our booming money markets. As David Hume put it, "It is easy for the rich, in an arbitrary government, to conspire against [the middle class], and to throw the whole burthen of the taxes on their shoulders."[17]

Some of you may say, "Well, perhaps we are in a corporatist society, but we do not have an arbitrary government." Of course we don't. But our governments can no longer decide tax levels on resident corporations. These are set arbitrarily by an abstract replacement for government called the global economy. The effective tax rate on large corporations throughout the West is now about 13 percent. I repeat, 13 percent. Raise that rate and they'll leave town. In other words, the taxation levels that used to be set by governments are now set by the global economy. So Hume's sentence should be rephrased to read, "It is easy for the transnationals, in an arbitrary global system, to conspire against [the middle class], and to throw the whole burthen of taxes on their shoulders."

Because the middle classes do not have enough money to fund the state, the result of this shift has been a decline in real tax revenue, followed by a rise in governmental debt and the cutting of public programs.

But what happens to the corporate money that is not taxed? If it were invested properly, perhaps the growth engendered would be worth society's sacrifice. Perhaps.

However, as I have already said, the managers have been wasting their corporations' massive incomes on such things as mergers and acquisitions, privatized public utilities which are unlikely to engender growth, to say nothing of their skyscrapers and high salaries.

Perhaps the most disturbing consequence of government's loss of corporate tax revenues has been the rise of publicly organized gambling. The hundreds of millions, in some countries billions, of dollars raised this way come in large part from the most discouraged part of the population. It's their choice, the cynical will say. But it is the governments of those citizens—governments constantly going on about the need for hard work and initiative—who suddenly are calling on those same citizens via vast advertising campaigns to "Escape the Jungle" for $2 with a possible return of $1,000. Or win "Instant Millions" for $5 with a possible return of $1 million.

This takes us back to the state lotteries prominent in the early Industrial Revolution. Governments, confused by the disorder in their society, turned to gambling to raise funds. As they are today, those lotteries were aimed at the less fortunate and less educated.

The most direct experience that the citizenry has with

globalization is in the area of unemployment and the declining value of employment. It is there that Destiny seems to ring most insistently. Apparently nothing can be done. Governments promise job creation, but as the official international bank of the central bankers (the Bank for International Settlements) put it in 1993: "Even unorthodox measures seem to have offered little remedy for the rising trend of unemployment."[18] The neo-conservatives cynically preach self-reliance when they know full well it can have little effect. What is the individual to do alone against a global system that brings large governments to their knees? The market disciples ignore the repeated admonition of their idol, Adam Smith, that high wages are essential to growth and prosperity. As he put it:

"The liberal reward of labour . . . is the natural symptom of increasing national wealth."

or

"But what improves the circumstances of the greater part can never be regarded as an inconveniency to the whole."

or

"Where wages are high, accordingly, we shall always find the workmen more active, diligent, and expeditious than where they are low."[19]

The market theorists also ignore the impossibility of continuing for very much longer with between 35 and 50 million unemployed in the West. These are not conditions in which a society can operate over any period of time. The Luddite burning of a few factories in the early nineteenth century was a local boiling over by frustrated victims of early mechanization. But it was also an unconscious general warning that such a situation could not continue.

Society chose to ignore the warning. In fact they hung five of the Luddites and transported the rest. By 1813 it was all over. Over in theory, that is. But what these rejected artisans had warned against—impossible work conditions, uncontrolled preference for technology over humans and a market-led society—resulted in almost two centuries of impossible social division. This produced both communism and fascism, to say nothing of an endless sequence of rebellions and civil wars. For 150 years street riots were a common occurrence and they usually ended with cavalry charges and volleys of rifle fire. Even the two greatest Western massacres—the two world wars—were the product of our inability to come to terms with this self-destructive social schism. At last, over the last half-century we have actually managed to defuse the worst of these divisions—a remarkable accomplishment, even if it was excruciatingly slow in coming.

To say now that the negative results of globalization are simply Destiny is to say that a whole new round of social divisions and violence is also our Destiny. In other words, the collapsing job market, slipping standards of living, the loss of fair regulations, the evaporation of big business tax revenues and the weakening of social programs are inevitable and so we must begin the endless, sterile battles of social division all over again.

> Ill fares the land, to hast'ning ills a prey,
> Where wealth accumulates, and men decay.

Oliver Goldsmith wrote his long, moving requiem to *The Deserted Village* in 1770, at the beginning of the first round of land use reorganization and industrialization in Britain. Our problems are theoretically far more complex, but we also have the sophisticated mechanisms to deal with them. All of the characteristics of globalization, which make it seem uncontrollable, in reality make it easy to control. Technology makes it easier than ever to enforce regulations. Policy standards are collapsing only because there is little agreement—except perhaps inside the European Union—between countries as to what standards there should be. This is not something technocrats can take the lead on. It is a matter of pure politics; that is, of citizens participating so they can demand multinational agreements.

The development of international trade agreements shows where the corporatist interest lies. These treaties also demonstrate that it is entirely possible to achieve concrete international agreements, filled with detailed regulations, which have a direct effect on the activities of the marketplace. The citizenry have made few efforts to push a more balanced agenda into their national arenas let alone onto the international level. Instead of haggling over local, complex and expensive punishment and reward systems, we could easily use our sophistication to develop simple, all-inclusive methods for guaranteeing standards of living. The Germans have perhaps been the most successful at doing this on a national level.

Hume quite rightly based his commercial economy upon the existence of "regular government."[20] The rule of law. His economy did not require democracy, but it did require regularity, stability and effective enforcement.

Every day we see how our superficially democratic but profoundly corporatist society suffers economically from the disorder of globalization; in other words, from the lack of regular government. The corporatists cannot deal with this. It is the old problem of using pure self-interest when broader disinterest is required. And only democracy can produce that kind of leadership.

Let me finish in comedy, or is it tragicomedy. The money markets are today treated as the fourth pillar of the new economics. This is now the most successful area of economic activity—the most successful in a very long time. Every day, currency traders move $1 trillion around the world.[21] This would seem to suggest that a lot of money is available. And that if a very small part of it were paid in taxes most of our public-financing problems would be solved.

There are, unfortunately, two impediments. This money is not available for taxation. And more importantly, it doesn't really exist. Money that bears no relationship to reality is imaginary. It is pure inflation. Hume:

> Money is not, properly speaking, one of the subjects of commerce; but only the instrument which men have agreed upon to facilitate the exchange of one commodity for another. It is none of the wheels of trade. It is the oil which renders the motion of the wheels more smooth and easy.[22]

Smith:

> Money is neither a material to work upon, nor a tool to work with.[23]

Those devoted to market forces tend not to mention Smith and Hume on the subject of money. The reason is very simple. The Chicago economists and their friends are in total self-contradiction on this very large subject. In fact, they have gone over to Smith's and Hume's enemies—the mercantilists—an economic movement which believed, among other things, that money was a value in itself. For that matter, they have also gone over to the mercantilists in their support of the transnationals, the modern version of the old royal monopolies. At first glance such enormous self-contradictions appear unbelievable. But that is only if you accept their claim to be free-market theorists. Their positions make much more sense when you realize that they are the corporatist theorists of a managerial society.

In the matter of money markets, it is Smith and Hume who are right. The explosion in these markets does not finance growth because money markets unrelated to financing real activity are pure inflation. And for that matter, they are a very esoteric, pure form of ideology. It is as if Mao had been reincarnated as a hedge fund manager and declared the theme of his financial revolution to be, "Let a thousand red suspenders bloom!"

A sign of this separation between money markets and economics is the interest rate conundrum. Since Smith and Hume—indeed all the way back to Athens—there has been general agreement that low interest rates usually produce growth. Abruptly, in the 1980s and 1990s, low interest rates began consistently to produce inflation. For two reasons. First, the economy is filled with unmeasured inflation, such as the money markets. Second, our lack of regulations in this whole area means that we encourage speculation. And in the final analysis, that's all the money markets are. Old-fashioned speculation run by sophisticated new technocrats. It is as if John Law had been reincarnated as something far worse than he had ever been and the South Sea Bubble made respectable. If society will permit and reward robbery, robbery will be invested in.

Precisely because the money markets are pure speculation, they are the easiest areas to regulate. Even basic agreements between OECD members could shut down large parts of this tumbling instability. It is claimed that Bretton Woods collapsed before the force of the marketplace. It could be answered that Bretton Woods—a first attempt at international monetary regulation—oversaw 30 years of remarkable growth with relatively low inflation and a few small crises. The unregulated money markets have now given us over twenty years of crisis, instability, gratuitous speculation and no real growth.

But is it growth that we need or want? Many social critics argue that we have had a period of growth so frenzied that it could not have helped but come to an end. They talk of the need for such things as sustainable development. As for the managerial, corporatist elites, they have remained true to their form. They are unable to see beyond their defined interests to any larger picture. For them, the larger picture exists only as an ideological abstract. In practical terms it does not exist.

They are fixated on the eighteenth- and nineteenth-century idea of growth, which more or less added up to the direct production of goods, in particular of capital goods.

However, our society seems unable to go any farther down that road. We have no need of more real production. Our elites have therefore set about inventing a fairy tale imitation of growth. Note that although a corporatist society discourages creativity, it encourages delusion. And on the subject of growth, what we are experiencing is a feeding frenzy of delusion. The money markets are a prime example. But so also are the commercial property booms; the endless investment in management structures; and our embroidering of consumerism which ranges from the highly baroque to the outright lunatic.

The deeper we plunge into this false growth, the more the economy itself becomes innately inflationary.

I would suggest that we are in desperate need of a reformulation of the idea of growth. The early industrial model is not working. Applied to our society it is an exclusionary formula. And the false growth encouraged by the technocracy is dragging us even deeper into crisis. Yet the ideals of sustainable development remain far removed from the realities of applied power.

For example, growth, as we currently understand it, classifies education as a cost, thus a liability. A golf ball, on the other hand, is an asset and the sale of it a measurable factor of growth. A face lift is an element of economic activity while a heart bypass is a liability which the economy must finance. Holidays are among the pearls of the service industry, while child care is a cost.

In other words, our concept of assets and liabilities, of goods versus expenses, has a negative effect on the realities of growth. We are unable to take into account the needs of a sophisticated society. Investment in training and in the care of citizens cannot be treated as an asset. Yet the illusion of growth through the sale of golf balls remains firmly in place.

It is difficult to imagine how we might escape our ongoing economic crisis unless we can reconsider the nature of growth. As you would expect in a corporatist society, our current narrow view is focused tightly on short-term interests. By reconsideration I mean that we must attempt to draw back far enough to see where value lies in the society. The more sophisticated the civilization, the more probable it is that value will lie in areas which are not of direct interest. If growth can be conceived in a wider, more inclusive form, then it will abruptly become possible to reward those things which society finds useful.

Our current obsession with the invisible hand of the marketplace is of no help in such a situation. It merely exacerbates our state of economic illusion and imbalance.

That which you are told today is the inevitable product of economic truth and globalization is more accurately the passive assertion of superstitious men waiting for Destiny to fell them. It is an attitude that most sensible men and women can easily reject. But rejection means assuming responsibility. And in our elites there is no desire to initiate changes which would insert the concept of responsibility into that of power. Only a persistent public commitment by the citizenry could bring such a thing about.

V

FROM IDEOLOGY
TOWARDS EQUILIBRIUM

ON THE DAY THAT YOU or I achieve a stable condition of equilibrium, those around us who have been less fortunate will draw one of two conclusions. Either that we are dead or that we have slipped into a state of clinically diagnosable delusion. And to live in delusion is to live in the comfort of ideology.

Practical humanism is the voyage towards equilibrium without the expectation of actually arriving there. Just as ideology stretches from the global to the miniature, so the non-ideological approach applies at every level. To begin with, there is Socrates' initial voyage—towards knowledge without the expectation of finding truth.

There is not, nor has there ever been, any sign of any invisible hands to hold us passively in a natural equilibrium. Human society is a human construct, even if outside

154

forces oblige, propel and limit us. Humanist society—that is, in our terms, the individual as citizen in a democratic society—is not only a human construct. It continues to exist only through the daily efforts of its citizenry.

I have already mentioned a number of oppositions central to this daily effort. We can now add to the list such simple battles as that for consciousness versus the comfort of remaining in the unconscious; responsibility versus passivity; doubt versus certainty; delight in the human condition or sympathy for the condition of others versus self-loathing and cynicism regarding the qualities of others.

This idea that sympathy for others is the essential characteristic of the human condition was, incidentally, central to Adam Smith's *Theory of Moral Sentiments,* a treatise that is rarely mentioned by the false disciples of his economic theories. They limit themselves to a narrow reading of *The Wealth of Nations* and then apply it to the general organization and conditions of society. There is no indication that that was what Smith intended.

After all, his theory of sympathy rejected self-love as the basic motive for behaviour. He also defined virtue as consisting of three elements: propriety, prudence and benevolence. By this he meant propriety or the appropriate control and directing of our affections; prudence or the judicious pursuit of our private interest; and benevolence or the exercise of only those affections that encourage the happiness of others. How poor Adam Smith got stuck with disciples like the market economists and the neo-conservatives is hard to imagine. He is in profound disagreement with their view of society.

Perhaps there is one other essential opposition that should be added to the list: the acceptance of time versus the fear of it. Ideology uses time as a weapon. It plays upon our fears of death or of ceasing to exist, which are largely unconscious. It scratches away indirectly at those fears by turning time into a recurrent bogeyman of the most practical aspects of the human condition. Time is limited. There's no time to lose.

The recurring delusion of a safe haven in both the grandiose and the microscopic aspects of our lives is tied to defeating time or at least to controlling it. The whole discourse of necessity and inevitability that surrounds the ideologies—from corporatism on down to the payment of debts—is constructed around a 'now or never' threat. Time, the great enemy, will defeat us if we hesitate for a moment to think or to doubt. Panicked, we flee towards certainty.

At the very origin of management theory lies the falsely scientific Taylorist model of the mechanistic human. The uncertainty of time, which surrounds human activity, is to be removed by encasing us in a structure fit for machinery. Machines may depreciate, but they do not fear death. As for the hierarchical structures of corporatism, they create an illusion of time eternally fixed in place. Here, in the role of a function, the human escapes the threat of time passing, except on an institutional level.

In the late twentieth century there is a curious, highly practical sidebar to this problem. Individuals have never had so much time. In this century alone Westerners have added some 25 years to their life expectancy. We now have 50 percent more time in which to do whatever we wish.

Given our general standard of living and our education, we could be using at least some of that time to think more and to replace the race to certainty with a more relaxed approach towards doubt.

Yet the actual effect of having 50 percent more time seems to have been the exact opposite. We have retreated further still into those unconscious fears that make us susceptible to the menace of time. Over the past few years the threats of necessity, of now or never, have repeatedly and with remarkable ease swayed highly sophisticated publics.

We could excuse ourselves by claiming that most of these great changes were tied to economic policy and that most of us are particularly ill-equipped to deal sensibly with these questions, given the quasi-unanimity in the community of economists. At least we have stood firm on questions of racism, where in the recent past we have been so weak.

But this is no excuse at all. When we acted badly over race there was quasi-unanimity in the relevant elites on that question. Each era has its ideologies and the citizen is rarely given a fair chance to consider questions. Our chance is what we make it.

Look, for example, at the manner in which we organize our lives today, from our education on through our careers. The pattern increasingly represents a desperate rush, as if driven by the threat that time will leave us behind. The result is that increasing percentages of our population are now faced by a quarter-century of inactivity. We call it retirement and part of it is welcome. But not 25 years. What this indicates is that, on the conscious level, there is no particular reason, and certainly no practical reason, for us to be front-end loading our lives. Then why does our civilization push us to do so?

Well, corporatism—with its market- and technology-led delusions—is profoundly tied to a mechanistic view of the human race. This is not an ideology with any interest in or commitment to the shape of society or the individual as citizen. It is fixed upon a rush to use machinery—inanimate or human—while these are still at full value; before they suffer any depreciation.

There is one opposition, very much on people's minds, that may appear to be missing from my list. What about the obligations of the individual versus her rights? This is the great subject dividing the Right from the Left or the neoconservatives from the liberals.

Not only have I not put these two terms forward in opposition, I have not used them till now in the habitual manner. Why? Because I believe that the manner in which we have come to use them is a severe deformation of the history of these concepts and therefore contributes to a repetitive, sterile debate. This debate in turn confirms the reign of corporatism and facilitates the victory of those who wish market forces and technology to lead our civilization. The fault for this misrepresentation lies as much on the Left as on the Right.

When those from the centre onwards to the Left talk about rights, it is as if these were free-standing and unrelated to the existence of society, which means unrelated to the existence of the public good. And from the centre on to the Right, obligations are invoked as if they referred either to a requirement to look after yourself in isolation from society or as a requirement to serve certain absolute needs of society, which usually come down to law and order, defence and moral order. Again, there is no suggestion of the shared role of the citizen in the maintenance of the public good.

The intellectual position of both Right and Left is thus similar because both are based upon a concept of individualism as self-absorption or selfishness. The Left, of course, would protest that these rights are equally distributed and therefore represent a form of fairness. They would also protest that they see government, regulation and taxation as making up the essential structure that enables society to function fairly. But if their definition of rights creates a form of individualism independent from that essential structure, well then, they have created the conditions for the aborting—both theoretical and practical—of the fair society they wished to create.

Look at the ease with which the institutions, regulations and programs designed to increase fairness are slipping away in our society. Surely this is the ultimate demonstration of the flaw in the reformers' approach.

As for the version of individualism advocated by the Right, it is the product of either naiveté or cynicism. What are they saying? That individualism requires the individual citizen to deny himself the use of his ability and his right to pool his strengths with those of other citizens through the public mechanisms of their own making. This is a maniacally self-destructive idea of human society. It abandons the individual to isolation before enormous, unpredictable and uncontrollable forces. Only a handful of people and their hangers-on are in a position to do well out of such an imbalanced confrontation. Not surprisingly, the hangers-on in question are those who busily sell the necessity of such an unbalanced confrontation. The reality of obligation, as it is presented to us today, is therefore one of loyalty—that is, of obedience—to the corporatist structures.

The origin of this deformed idea of obligation is relatively simple to trace. It goes back to the birth of the corporatist movement around 1870, when religious leaders and established hierarchical interests were looking for a way in which to accept industrialization while denying individualism and democracy. Their solution was to combine and restructure the old concept of the faithful servant of God and the dutiful subject of social authority in order to create the obligated subject of rational corporatist structures.

The origins of the Left's interpretation of the citizen's rights is rather more complicated. From the twelfth century on, and in particular from the seventeenth century on, the battle by the citizenry and their allies to liberate themselves from their artificial status as subjects has been extremely difficult. It has been even more difficult for them to formalize their position as the source of legitimacy. I use the word "battle" because advances have been won only after great struggle and over a very long period of time, well on into the second half of the twentieth century.

The reality of this struggle unfortunately took on a form that undermined the intent. By focusing upon the taking away of rights, one after the other, from the established order, the forces of reform confirmed in practice what they denied in theory. In theory they talked about natural rights.

In practice these rights were presented as having been won from the established order. The source of legitimacy therefore remained unchanged. The rights had merely been temporarily removed from the established order by force. Today, those same rights are slipping effortlessly back into the hands of the corporatist form of that established order. And this is happening in spite of endless formal declarations of citizens' rights.

Why? Because the reality of the citizen as the source of legitimacy has never been successfully formalized in practice. Why? Because the rights won were defined by the forces of reform as free-standing rights—free-standing, that is, from the old order. This meant, unfortunately, that they would also be free-standing from the formalization of the citizen's defence of those rights—that is, from the public good.

On top of this, today's inheritors of the leadership of the reform movement have consolidated their idea of rights into their own acceptance of corporatist structures. To take just one example, philosophy has always been central to the public debate over the human condition. This is because successful reform depends upon a widespread understanding of the philosophical options available and of their implications. Suddenly, the great philosophical voice of humanist decency is absent from the public debate. Why? Because most of its exponents are caught up in the complexities of philosophical professionalism—a world of narrow specializations and impenetrable dialect. A corporation of philosophy. They have left the field of public debate wide open to more cynical forces on the other side. How can those who share the humanist approach be led by people who do not believe that philosophical public debate is possible? Let alone worthwhile?

I could trace this phenomenon through sector after sector; in other words, through corporation after corporation. The liberal and social democratic thinkers have all too often chosen what they see as the high ground of specialization and professionalism. The real populism of citizen-based legitimacy and public debate has been abandoned to the false populism of the old order.

I would like to mention one last source of the Left's weakness. From the beginnings of the Enlightenment there has been among the reformers at least the hint of a fear of the citizen. The liberals in particular have been devoted to the citizen in theory, but not really to the citizen in flesh and bone and in mind.

And so the movement for citizens' rights has been seen as an ideal, put in place from above or outside. In essence, the Socratic movement has been infected from the beginning by the Platonists' distrust of the populace. Or to fit this problem into the modern experience, the reforming elites have never been able to free themselves entirely from the authoritarian campaign initiated by Hobbes in the seventeenth century. He argued that the populace would run amok unless kept in awe of some sort of authority. And fear of punishment was the best way to control us. Our reforming elites have rejected the most blatant aspects of Hobbes' fear-mongering to keep us in our place, but accepted almost entirely his view of social organization as a control mechanism. In the *Leviathan,* Hobbes put it that "during the time men live without a common power to keep them all in awe, they are in that condition which is called war." The citizen's rights have been buried in law and the citizen's status in the hierarchy of professionalism.

To the extent that legal and professional organization lacks the emotional power to keep us in cowed, we have added the force of ideology. Who would not be cowed by the "invisible hand" of the marketplace or the "manifest destiny" of technology? But it is law and hierarchy combined which create the form of a controlled society. The reformers saw this control as being exercised in the name of justice, but their approach has left us undefended before the forces of self-interest.

Look at the eagerness with which liberal and social democratic governments are embracing the idea that general schooling should be restructured to act as a direct conduit to the managerial economy. You will find this idea popping up throughout the West. The new Italian centre-left coalition is the latest example. They all say: "We must be practical. We must produce citizens who can find jobs." But these changes will not help individuals in the work place. They will, however, prepare the young to accept the structures of corporatism.

Well then, if the debate over the individual's rights versus the individual's obligations has been so defined as to be sterile and even dangerous for democracy, can either term be sensibly reformulated?

I would use them this way. The individual's rights are guaranteed by law only to the extent that they are protected by the citizenry's exercise of their obligation to participate in society. Rights are a protection from society. But only by fulfilling their obligations to society can the individual give meaning to that protection.

What then of an educational and social system which believes passionately that professionalism and specialization are central to raising the human species above the morass of superstition and emotion; and that this can only be done through a narrow, goal-oriented education and through action based on expertise? None of this can be lightly dismissed. It feeds our elites across the political spectrum.

But this is an abstract approach to society, and humans do not function as an abstraction. Power lies in the mechanisms that make the whole function. This abstract view of society denies that power to humans. An educational or social system that defines progress as the total of a myriad of more or less water-tight compartments denies the possibility of a citizen-based society. It therefore denies the individual as the source of legitimacy.

However fine the abstract intentions of professionalism and expertise may be, the net result of this approach is a mechanistic view of men and women. Knowledge and understanding in their real sense—as the foundations of consciousness—become impossible. Society conceived in this way is viewed through corporatist eyes and denies both the complexity of the human and the complexity of human society.

Real individualism then is the obligation to act as a citizen. This has nothing to do with conformism or obedience to interests outside of the public good. Let me repeat for a last time a few lines from Socrates' self-defence:

> Perhaps someone may say, "But surely, Socrates, after
> you have left us you can spend the rest of your life in
> quietly minding your own business." This is the hard-
> est thing of all to make some of you understand. If I say
> that . . . I cannot "mind my own business," you will not
> believe [me].

Now the very essence of corporatism is minding your own business. And the very essence of individualism is the refusal to mind your own business. This is not a particularly pleasant or easy style of life. It is not profitable, efficient, competitive or rewarded. It often consists of being persistently annoying to others as well as being stubborn and repetitive. The German voice of the Enlightenment, Friedrich Nicolai, put it clearly: "Criticism is the only helpmate we have which, while disclosing our inadequacies, can at the same time awake us to the desire for greater improvement."[1]

Criticism is perhaps the citizen's primary weapon in the exercise of her legitimacy. That is why, in this corporatist society, conformism, loyalty and silence are so admired and rewarded; why criticism is so punished or marginalized. Who has not experienced this conflict?

In one eloquent example which has recently come to light, the executives of a major American tobacco company debated among themselves at great length, in the 1960s, whether they should inform the U.S. Surgeon General of the results of their own corporate research, which confirmed the health hazards of smoking. They decided, eventually, to say nothing and to stop work on a safer cigarette. After all, to develop a safer cigarette would compromise their silence by suggesting the need for one. Instead, they initiated a legal and public relations strategy of admitting nothing.[2]

Their hard-debated decision not to criticize actually forced them to go in the exact opposite direction, towards aggressive conformity.

> The fault, dear Brutus, is not in our stars,
> But in ourselves, that we are underlings.

The fault lies also in the corporatist structures. The tobacco executives did avoid Brutus' fate for a time, although only by sacrificing their self-respect; that is, by abandoning individualism in order to remain underlings. Now fate has overtaken them and in addition they have lost their honour; they have lost the public face of the self-respect the system had encouraged them to abandon 30 years earlier.

It isn't surprising in such an atmosphere of professional conformism that we should seek release in what I would call false individualism. It could also be called superficial self-satisfaction. The problem is not that looking after our personal desires is innately wrong. Clothes, holidays, sports, multiple marriages and orgasms, face and other lifts can be agreeable diversions on life's tiring road. Why shouldn't we divert ourselves? The problem is that these agreeable moments are increasingly identified as the expression of individualism. As individualism itself.

The private-sector managerial class and the neo-conservatives in particular complain that the poor have been given self-serving rights; yet they themselves embrace the self-serving rights of pleasure with enthusiasm.

Not only is there nothing wrong with these distractions, if kept in perspective, but it is also normal in a society that a percentage of the population should want to walk away from any involvement whatsoever. The freedom of that small minority not to participate is a sign of the society's health. But you know a society is in trouble when the virtual totality of the elite, now a good third of the population, adopts public silence and private passivity on the professional level, then walks away from society to blow off accumulated steam on private pleasures.

There is a certain satisfaction in personal release, but as one of Albert Camus' characters put it: *Un homme, ça s'empêche. Voilà ce qu'est un homme, ou sinon . . .*[3] A man controls himself. That's what a man is, if not . . ."

Our problem is not choosing whether to abolish pleasure or to embrace it, but to find mechanisms that might help release the individual from the conformity of corporatism.

We know exactly what does happen when the citizen does participate; we've known since the rise of juries in the early Middle Ages. In the process of seeking agreement among themselves, these disinterested, unrelated groups of twelve usually discover within themselves a mixture of strengths through the various human qualities. The jury thus becomes a mechanism of equilibrium. Its human balance provides something that escapes the judge and the expert witnesses. You will note that their task is not to find the answer, not to find the truth, but to establish whether or not there is reasonable doubt. This is the role of the citizen personified.

One of our greatest needs today is to find ways, even

simple mechanisms, that will help us, the citizenry, to get into the public debate in such a manner as to duplicate the conscious understanding of the jury. We are not going to defeat or overthrow or even abandon the corporatist structure, in spite of its failures. This is a system that continually grows stronger while the society it controls grows weaker. It is therefore a matter of inserting the citizen as citizen into the system in whatever way we can. And then letting the mechanisms of criticism combined with high levels of involvement take effect.

How can this be done? Well, consider the formalized dynamics of our civilization. Corporatist society has structured itself so as to eliminate citizen participation in public affairs, except through the isolated act of voting and through voluntary activities. These voluntary activities involve sacrificing time which has been put aside, formally, for other activities. Thus sports, meals, holidays, to say nothing of work, are actually structured into our financial and social reward system. Citizen participation is not. In fact, almost everything we do—except our participation as citizens—is formally structured into our social system. This suggests that in a corporatist society democracy is formally discouraged. It is marginalized into volunteerism. And yet, by simply formalizing the citizen's participation—that is, by setting aside a certain number of hours a week through our structuring of the official activities of the individual—we would be able to launch large numbers of people into public activity. What effect they would have cannot be judged in advance. But in a society obsessed by structure, we would have officially recognized the mainstream function of criticism, non-conformism and disinterest.

It would be impossible for the corporatist structure itself ever to reward or admire criticism. The necessity therefore is to reinforce the plane on which criticism can prosper and eventually enable the citizen to dominate.

But even this simple role of criticism will remain an impossible ideal unless we are able to consciously identify how far we have slipped—as citizens—into verbal conformism. Perhaps if we can learn to compare our approach to public debate with that of our predecessors—the Christians of the early Middle Ages, for example—we may be able to recognize our passivity. The medieval heretic was someone who "showed intellectual arrogance by preferring his own opinions to those who were specially qualified to pronounce upon matters of faith." In place of "faith" you could today insert any one of our thousands of specializations. "Consequently heresy was high treason, committed against the divine Majesty. . . ."[4] We have progressed in our control of high treason. We no longer need to draw and quarter. The heretic today merely finds his career shattered and himself cast to the margins of corporatist society.

The citizen's great difficulty in making public debate work begins, however, with the crisis in our language. I have talked about the division between the powerless public language and the rhetoric, propaganda and dialects of corporatism. The resulting blockage in public debate is enormous. There is a desperate need to deal with the simplest of communication problems—for a start, with the nonsense factor in official language.

Our underlying problem is that public language can no longer shape power by fighting single, isolated causes. This method of public debate was introduced in the eighteenth century. Today, the seamless web of corporatism means that these specific battles for justice end up at best as isolated victories, which are often then easily marginalized. The old spreading effect of a just cause is now far more difficult to accomplish.

When I talk about the necessity to make nonsense of official language, I am referring to our need to discredit a whole approach to language. One small example: it would be a major accomplishment if we were able to focus on the tendency of those, who make the arguments for corporatism, to also praise the rural idyll—*Italia Rurale*, as Mussolini put it. Or small-town America. Or common-sense conservatism. Always behind these simplistic utopias is a sense of moral cleanliness, deep roots, local belonging, clarity of shared vision; all the things which the proposers of these simple utopias are removing with their other hand through corporatism.

Such a two-handed approach is so contradictory as to be ridiculous. But the difficulty of expressing the corporatist problem, as against the simplicity of expressing the false utopia, makes one a perfect foil for the other. As a result we seem unable to identify the comic nature of the official discourse.

And yet there is nothing new about this trickery. Émile Durkheim laid out the corporatist method clearly a hundred years ago. The real information, he said, was too complex for people.

It can only become a public possession through the circulation of symbols which, because they are "simple, definite, and easily representable," render intelligible a truth which, "owing to its dimensions, the number of its parts, and the complexity of their arrangement, is difficult to hold in mind."[5]

Durkheim spoke happily of symbols as propaganda. Symbols are the images of language which, used as values in themselves, are easily manipulable. We have moved away from the symbols and images of race, but we are still subject to their sway in the domain of power. Jung said that "the psyche consists essentially of images," and we are now in a civilization drowning under the impact of images. We have so far been unable to identify consciously the role those images can and do play as a tool of authority.

The manipulation of images is open to all of us. But it is the funded propagandist who can most easily and effectively use them. And even used honestly, the image is at best a symbol. It does not replace the ongoing communication of a functioning language.

It is through language that we will find our way out of our current dilemma, just as a rediscovery of language provided a way out for Westerners during the humanist breakthrough that began in the twelfth century. For those addicted to concrete solutions, this call for a rebirth or rediscovery of meaning may well seem vague and unrelated to reality. But language, when it works, is the tool that makes it possible to invoke reality.

Before Benjamin Franklin began to think about lightning,

the received wisdom had it identified as a supernatural phenomenon. For that reason, gunpowder was often stored in
churches, to give it divine protection. Church bells were
rung during thunderstorms to ward off the bad spirits.
Between 1750 and 1784, lightning struck 386 German
churches, killing 103 bell-ringers.[6] In 1767 lightning struck a
Venetian church whose vaults were filled with gunpowder.
The explosion killed 3,000 people.

   In other words, there was ample proof that divine protection did not ward off lightning. But so long as there was no
language to destroy the received wisdom, it remained in
place. Our experiences today with the invisible hand of the
marketplace are similar. What we require is the language to
demonstrate its comic nature. Between 1973 and 1995, how
often has the lightning of economic catastrophe struck Western economies? Where was the divine protection of the
invisible hand? Franklin demonstrated the true nature of
lightning by thinking about the problem, constructing an
argument and finally subjecting it to practical experiment.

   The difficulty with many of the arguments used today to
examine reigning fallacies is that they have fallen into the
general assumptions of deconstructionism. They do not seek
meaning or knowledge or truth. They seek to demonstrate
that all language is tied to interest. The deconstructionists
have argued against language as communication in order to
get at the evils of rhetoric and propaganda. But if language
is always self-interest, then there is no possibility of disinterest and therefore no possibility of the public good. The net
effect has been to reinforce the corporatist point of view that
we all exist as functions within our corporations.

To rephrase this problem in terms of my argument, the deconstructionists have effectively attacked our addiction to answers, but in such a way as to undermine the validity of our questions. And so the answers, assertive as they are, stand reinforced.

In any case, the best hope for a regeneration of language lies not in academic analysis but in citizen participation. We know that the universities are in crisis and are attempting to ride out the storm by aligning themselves with various corporatist interests. That is short-sighted and self-destructive. From the point of view of their obligation to society, it is simply irresponsible.

But the universities are also in crisis because the historic process of learning has slipped, once again, back into the comfortable cubbyhole of sophism and scholasticism. In the fifth century B.C., the Sophists aimed at producing not wisdom or goodness, but efficiency and cleverness.[7] This may sound familiar; these are characteristics vaunted by the business schools and those parts of the social sciences that feed the think tanks and foundations.

Socrates asked Hippocrates, "Wouldn't you be ashamed to show yourself to the Greeks as a Sophist?" Hippocrates replied, "Yes, truly, Socrates, if I am to say what I think."

As for the scholastics, from the sixteenth century on, what we remember of them was their ability to tie up any arguments that might relate to reality in a perpetual process of marginalia. All available time was used up on intellectual procedures and interpretation. This required intelligence, but it did not require thought.

The situation today within our highly sophisticated and

fractured fields of learning is very much the same. We can only discuss or make intellectual advances by passing through the existing body of learning. This is such an enormous task, made even more enormous by the multitudes of specialized gate keepers, that no one can produce integrated thought. Such intellectual splintering explains some of academia's passivity before the crisis of the society they ought to be defending.

It simply isn't good enough for philosophers, political scientists and economists—three fields particularly relevant to the democratic system—to protest that complexity makes serious integrated public debate of their issues impossible. Surely they have noticed that the remarkable public support they have had through much of this century and, indeed, back through the nineteenth century, has been falling away. To what do they attribute this? I would identify a sense in the citizenry that they have been abandoned by their thinkers; a sense of being betrayed by an intelligentsia which does not take the humanist experience seriously, particularly not the drama of the citizen-based democracy.

The sensible thing for the university community to do now would be to turn away from its self-interest in order to take on a leadership role in the movement to reinvigorate and broaden pre-university education. They might discover that disinterested action of this sort would strengthen the role of the universities by pulling them away from collaboration with the corporatist model. Back towards the wider obligations of humanism.

This approach and my earlier comment on how to insert the citizenry into the formal system of power are intended to indicate that our need is not, at this time, for another round of incremental changes in one direction or another. The effects of corporatism are so invasive that the strategy of the citizenry should be to change not the policies in place but the dynamics.

Let me give you another example. I spoke earlier in this chapter about our panicked front-end loading of education and careers onto relatively long lives. Not only does the system demand a rushed process, it demands an increasingly specialized process.

We are already suffering from the effects of university graduates who have little or no basic education because the requirements of the job market were so directly quantified in the courses required for their degrees. Now that same phenomenon is reaching down into pre-university education.

Yet our real problem is not one of time. It will be increasingly one of finance. Over the long term, no society will be able to finance 25 to 35 years of retirement. It would be far more sensible—and far more liveable for the individual—to re-examine our outdated patterns. Why not take five to ten years from the end of a life and transfer it to the beginning? In other words, why not actually make some use of the time won through longer life expectancy? And I don't mean mere utilitarian use. If a 50 percent increase in longevity is a victory for civilization, then it is civilization which should gain some advantage from it.

For example, there is absolutely no need to narrow the spectrum of pre-university education in order to focus on structural elements such as management and technology. And there is no need for universities to turn out 21-year-old specialists equipped with no memory of their civilization's experience, no ethical context, no sense of the larger shape of their society. At both levels there is ample time for a general education before turning to specialization. There is also ample time for serious periods of experience in public service before entering into 30 or 35 years of career.

The technocrat will say that we can't afford more education and more public service. The truth is that neither, from a humane or a financial point of view, can we afford to dump ourselves as individuals into limbo at age 55 or 60. As I have already pointed out, education is an asset not a liability. We see it as an unfinanceable cost only because of our narrow, outdated definition of growth.

We have everything to gain, even financially, by shrinking the size of public education classes—which means more teachers—and by broadening the scope of that education. And we need to take the time to give a solid undergraduate humanist education to future business students, medical students and economists, just to name a few categories, before allowing them to narrow their minds through specialization. This would have an important impact on their approach once they were unleashed on society. For one thing, it would strengthen their sense of existing, outside of their professions, as individual, responsible citizens. For another, it would feed their ability to think instead of clinging onto process.

As for the question of public service, we can see around us the gradual suffocation of citizen-based democracy. Why would we expect individuals who have been pushed at high speed into the corporatist process to change course, abruptly, at the height of their careers in order to become non-conforming, outspoken, disinterested citizens? We are getting precisely what we are creating. There is no longer any reason to blame this utilitarian or mechanistic approach on a lack of time. We now have long periods of free time at the end of our lives which if transferred to the early stages could be devoted to public service.

What public service? How would it be organized? Those are managerial questions. The place to begin is with the more basic questions of need, advantage and viability. If we can focus on these, the details will follow.

Each way we look, the need is not for reforms but for a change in dynamics. The same is true in politics. So long as money is a central element in political life, the largest interests will be able to use it for their own ends. The need therefore is not to limit finances or to fiddle with the monitoring of finances but simply to remove them from the electoral process. The floods of indirect propaganda from the visual technologies make all attempts at incremental reform counter-productive. But if the private-sector financing element were removed, what would remain would be a minimalist use of language and debate. The result would be a lower-key form of politics, one in which questioning and doubt were possible.

There are numerous schemes for limiting the effects of the runaway money markets—for example through transaction taxes. But that is another example of the self-defeating nature of incremental reforms. Such taxes would simply tie governments to a dependent relationship with the enemies of the real economy and of growth. On the other hand, a few simple joint agreements, even among a handful of Western governments, could actually shut down the most harmful parts of the speculation that rages about us.

Equally, the globalization arguments insist on the unregulable nature of all social policy in a new world without economic borders. This is manifestly untrue. A series of international binding trade agreements of great complexity have been signed over the past few years. Absolutely nothing prevents the negotiation of matching agreements on job equity and social standards. Nor is there any need for such agreements to begin at the all-inclusive international level. Like trade, social policy can first be established on a regional basis. What is described as the impossibility of international, social regulation is actually the unwillingness of the corporatist elites to enter into such negotiations. It is therefore a pure question of political will; that is, of democratic will.

Even in as vast an area as technology, our passivity is unnecessary. The only controls we have on new technology relate to various aspects of safety. But the addition of a public-interest component to those safety-oriented licensing agencies would bring a much calmer, more responsible attitude to technological change. The problem is not what science can discover, or applied science can develop, but whether we are willing to blindly subject our civilization to the abstract demigod of inanimate objects.

One way of examining our dynamics and how they might be changed is to ask ourselves what it is that we reward and punish in our society. I think you would be surprised if you drew up your own lists to discover that most of what we reward works against the public good and most of what we discourage or even punish would work in its favour.

I have spoken from the beginning about our slippage into the unconscious and our susceptibility to imbalance. We could call this the unconsciousness of imbalance or unbalanced unconsciousness. They feed each other. But if a society insists upon rewarding primarily that which weakens it and punishing that which can strengthen it, surely it is a clinically identifiable victim of both imbalance and the unconscious.

And so if our best hope to rectify this situation lies not in incremental reforms but in changes to our dynamic, so our ability to understand that dynamic lies in our ability to use our consciousness and to move towards some sort of equilibrium.

But surely a concept like equilibrium is soft and vague and far removed from the realities of unemployment and global competition? Not really. Our inability to see those relatively simple problems as other than uncontrollable conundrums comes in large part from our inability to use our various qualities, as a jury might. A jury attacks problems by the route of reasonable doubt. It is also reasonable doubt that makes it entirely possible to imagine a change in dynamics, such as formalized participation by the citizenry or money markets reduced to utility.

This idea of equilibrium is not new. Like so much else it has been with us in a recognizable form since Athens. Thinkers have always sought to identify either the components of the human condition or the qualities upon which humans can call.

Not surprisingly, what interested Plato were the components of the human condition. The ideologue is interested in that to which humans must submit. Plato said there were three components: first, the rational; then, courage or the passionate; and finally, something that could be called emotion or sensual appetite—hunger, thirst, sexual desire. These three components—the rational, courage and the sensual—made up the psyche. No human could escape from them. We could use them in balance or fall victim to one or the other or use each at appropriate moments.

The medieval churches' faith, hope and charity could also be seen as characteristics of the human condition. They were inescapable. They imposed passivity. They had been infused in us by God.

On the other hand, the four cardinal virtues of Hellenistic thought were an attempt to identify the qualities upon which humans could call in the various situations of life: justice, temperance, prudence, fortitude. Thomas Aquinas seized upon these in the Middle Ages and identified them as the "political virtues" or the "human virtues."[8] Faith, hope and charity were supranatural and thus inescapable. Justice, temperance, prudence and fortitude were available for the human to make use of in the interests of the greater good. Remember Adam Smith's moral treatise, which I mentioned earlier. He based human relationships upon sympathy, one for the other. But he based the exercise of that sympathy on three virtues: propriety, prudence and benevolence. You can see how heavily influenced he was by Aquinas. And once again you can see how profoundly

Smith would have detested the Chicago School of Economics and the neo-conservatives.

St. Augustine before Aquinas had identified three qualities: memory, reason and will. But what interested all of the humanist thinkers was the ability of the individual to somehow use his talents in some sort of equilibrium. It was the ability to balance her actions which made the human a human.

"We know the good," Euripides wrote, "but do not practise it." The true characteristic of consciousness is therefore not simply knowledge, but a balanced use of our qualities so that what we know and say is related to what we do. The humanist at his best proceeds through the best possible equilibrium. It is a balancing act that makes the narrow certainty of ideologies impossible.

Jung seemed alternately optimistic and pessimistic about whether this was possible. "Nature . . . is not so lavish with her boons that she joins to high intelligence the gifts of the heart also."[9] Among the Christian humanists of this century, Thomas Merton perhaps expressed the conflict best: "To live as a rational animal does not mean to think as a man and to live as an animal. We must both think and live as men."

As for these lists of qualities, it has always seemed to me that our ancestors were overly obsessed by the various mystical significances of the number three. Surely the miracle of humanism has the right to at least double the qualities of a triangle.

All the same, such a list can't help but be influenced by the precedents. And identifying its components is fraught with at least two types of dangers. One: slipping into what are essentially the platonic or religious characteristics of our condition; the characteristics to which we must submit. That is the danger of becoming an unconscious ideologue. Two: misinterpreting as fundamental qualities those characteristics that are the product of applying our qualities.

Thus some would argue that compassion is a fundamental human quality. I would say that, yes, it is an essential expression of our humanism. But it is produced by our fundamental qualities when they are functioning in a relatively successful equilibrium. As for hatred of ourselves or others—what I would call self-loathing or intolerance—that is the product of disequilibrium.

It seems to me that a sensible list of the human qualities would run as follows: common sense, creativity or imagination, ethics (not morality), intuition or instinct, memory and, finally, reason.

I have arranged all six in alphabetical order because I do not believe that equilibrium is aided by attempts to create orders of importance or precedence.

Those of you who have suffered from the misuse of terms such as intuition and common sense—for example, used as a cover for superstition and ignorance—may insist that neither of them belongs on any list of basic human qualities. For a start, they cannot exist as qualities because they cannot be accurately defined.

But none of these six terms is definable. Reason, for example, has been defined in thousands of ways by highly competent philosophers, as well as by professors of philosophy. These definitions have brought us no closer to a rational use of our rationality or to a humanistic use of our rationality. And the term—rational—has been used in this century as often, if not more often, than common sense, creativity, ethics, intuition or memory in order to justify acts of terrible injustice.

In other words, these qualities cannot be defined usefully, but only as abstractions, which they are not. A quality is directly applicable to reality. It can only be understood through use and misuse. That is why I took the time in an earlier chapter to ridicule the technical division of reason into two parts: reason as the godhead of all human considerations and instrumental reason as the shadow of the godhead.

Of course, each quality is permanently open for examination and discussion. But none can be fixed on a pedestal by an intellectual exercise. They are not defined in their true sense by the tools of the lexicographer, but through their relationship to each other. Set in juxtaposition one to the other and used in some sort of balance, each takes on a certain relief of its own and can be seen to make sense.

These qualities are the basic tools of humanity. In more aggressive verbiage, they are our weapons for use in what can only be described as a constant war against ideology. And therein lies the key to our unconscious self-loathing. Any one of these qualities, taken away from the others and used as an absolute value in itself, becomes a tool of ideology.

Look back over our litany of unfortunate experiences: churches invoking *ethics* as the source of their legitimacy received from God; absolute monarchs claiming the right to legitimacy through *memory*—i.e., through genealogy; revolutionaries claiming the magic of *creativity* to legitimize their ripping apart of what for the majority may have been an acceptable situation; *instinct* being used as the key that opens the door to the superiority of a race; *common sense* used to justify the most blatant applications of crude self-interest; and *reason,* in its most recent deformation, being used to justify corporatism itself, a system built around the dehumanization of the individual citizen.

Think of the twin French myths of abstract rationality and romantic memory struggling for a century against the German romantic myths of instinct and memory. When, after the Second World War, finally enough blood had been spilled, the two sides stood back and, in a fit of consciousness, abruptly recognized the non-exclusive nature of their myths. I think you could argue that the Franco-German alliance of the last 40 years has been a remarkably successful application of human qualities. Memory is still there, as is rationality and instinct. But these three qualities have been balanced against each other. And a strong element of common sense has been added, as well as some ethics. I think you could say there has not been enough ethics. And the absence of the imagination in this arrangement keeps these closest of partners almost artificially apart. Still, the multiplicity of the qualities engaged has made it the success that it is.

There are those who believe that there can never be enough of one quality or another. Ethics, for example—how could it need to be limited by other influences? Well, ask those who have been martyred by the ethical certainty of movements such as the Red Brigade. There are others who attach themselves fervently to reason. But they choose to forget its history. Let me quote for a last time that most impor-

tant of anti-democratic, anti-humanist voices, Émile
Durkheim: "The other task for the corporation consists in the
delegitimization of common sense."[10] In favour of what? In
favour of reason, which is the invoked deity of corporatism.

Or here is John Stuart Mill:

> The notion that truths external to the human mind may
> be known by intuition or consciousness . . . is, I am per-
> suaded, in these times, the great intellectual support of
> false doctrines and bad institutions. . . . There never was
> such an instrument devised for consecrating all deep-
> seated prejudices.[11]

True. Yet consider the international money markets.
These are the inventions of creativity at its most irresponsible and vacuous. And they operate with the most intricate of
rational skills. Common sense or ethics or even the memory
of past speculative booms ought to have been invoked
against this dangerous disorder. What is coming, bit by bit,
is an intuitive reaction from the public who, although they
have been allowed to understand little of what is going on,
nevertheless sense that we are slipping down a dangerously
delusionary road. They sense that this complex global market cannot be a limitless abstraction; that in a normal world
there is always room for some speculation. But a speculation
frenzy cannot end well. It is as if some athletes had taken to
eating, drinking and dancing all night. Their game would
suffer.

As for memory, it is perhaps the first quality that differen-
tiates us from the marketplace and from inanimate

machines. Neither has any memory. We, on the other hand, if we use our consciousness, can know what we have already done and what the effects were. The French novelist, Le Clézio, says that "art consists in bringing the memory of things past to the surface. But the author is not a *passéiste*, a worshipper of the past. He is linked to history—to memory—which is linked to the common dream." That common dream is part of the public good. It is the disinterested past, which acts both as a warning and a guide.

Certainly the highly rational qualities of those in the financial markets have not helped them towards a balanced attitude. Giambattista Vico complained in the early eighteenth century that reason was "a philosophy of judgement."[12] Vico saw the need for a greater use of memory, common sense and ethics. Certainly, it is that judgemental self-assurance of reason on its own that allows an economy of pure speculation to grow and prosper. Yet it is also the judgemental force of reason, properly used in context with other qualities, that allows us to make sense of our memory and our instincts.

What I have described in these five chapters is a civilization—our civilization—locked in the grip of an ideology—corporatism. An ideology that denies and undermines the legitimacy of the individual as the citizen in a democracy. The particular imbalance of this ideology leads to a worship of self-interest and a denial of the public good. The quality that corporatism claims as its own is rationality. The practical effects on the individual are passivity and conformism in the areas that matter and non-conformism in the areas that don't.

I spoke in the first pages of our need to escape the utopian nightmare—our own particular utopian nightmare. From within our situation, this seems impossible. Thomas Jefferson, one of the most successful politicians of the modern era and a man who, though full of faults like the rest of us, sought an equilibrium as best he could, put it that a great deal lay in the manner in which you approached reality. If the approach was balanced, "the knot which you thought a Gordian one will untie itself before you."[13] The very juxtaposition of our qualities produces in and of itself powers that cannot be intellectually identified by normal analysis, but which clarify our situation and open clearer avenues for action. Jung and Freud might call this the power of consciousness. I would call it the power of equilibrium.

Recently I saw a physical realization of this balance in the very southern tip of Korea, near the old royal capital of Kyongju. On the edge of a river in a deep mountain valley a great Confucian teacher, Yi Ŏn-chŏck, built himself a retirement house when he left government service in 1516. The five Confucian qualities with which until then he had governed other men were Wen, Ren, Chunzi, Li and De. They are the arts of peace; of goodness; of superior behaviour, which is the opposite of the petty and mean; of propriety or grace; and finally, of the just use of power. As you can see, these are surprisingly similar to our own view of human qualities.

The house he built is an expression of those qualities. When I came upon it I was immobilized without being able to identify the cause. At first, I had not even consciously seen the house. It wasn't so much a matter of its modesty and integration into the place, although it had both. There was no hint of the man's ego. No sense of his having built as opposed to having found a way to be part of the place. But the longer I looked, the more I could see something which expressed itself as harmony. Grace, yes, but harmony above all in its own terms and in those of nature. The materials, the lines of the myriad of freestanding walls, the roof lines, all swam into the surrounding land, the rocks, the river bed. The walls combined layers of boulders, flat tiles and unbaked clay, thus combining the mountains with sophisticated human skills as well as with the surrounding earth. Even the pavilions behind the walls had a sense to them that was not immediately apparent. Yet as I walked through the passageways it was as if the human flowed from one to the other in a discreet sonnet.

I am not suggesting that we should seek to live at the level of harmony achieved by a great Confucian teacher. Or even that harmony is appropriate to the democratic balance. But the constant movement towards equilibrium is.

What I found in that house was an expression—his expression—of balanced individualism. Ours is far more rough and tumble. It depends upon the commitment of the citizen to the common good. This is the true meaning of obligation. Those who govern or have power cannot on the one hand invoke obligation and on the other deny the common good and the real legitimacy of the citizen.

That great public figure, Wilfrid Laurier, who later in his life set in motion the process that would eventually bring all of the colonial empires to an end, stood up in the days

immediately after the Métis Rebellion and the hanging of
Louis Riel and said:

> What is hateful . . . is not rebellion but the despotism
> which induces the rebellion; what is hateful are not
> rebels but the men, who, having the enjoyment of
> power, do not discharge the duties of power; they are
> the men who, having the power to redress wrongs,
> refuse to listen to the petitioners that are sent to them;
> they are the men who, when they are asked for a loaf,
> give a stone.[14]

These words apply today with great precision to the corporatist leaders who, when they are called upon to deal with
the 50-odd million modern Luddites and our dropping standards of living, plead the inevitabilities of globalization as
well as the invisible hand of the marketplace and technology.

Equilibrium, in the Western experience, is dependent not
just on criticism, but on non-conformism in the public place.
The road away from the illusions of ideology towards reality is passable only if that anti-conformism makes full use of
our qualities and strengths in order to maintain the tension
of uncertainty. The examined life makes a virtue of uncertainty. It celebrates doubt.

Common sense, creativity, ethics, intuition, memory and
reason. These can be exploited individually as a justification
for ideology; or imprisoned in the limbo of abstract concepts. Or they can be applied together, in some sort of equilibrium, as the filters of public action.

The virtue of uncertainty is not a comfortable idea, but then a citizen-based democracy is built upon participation, which is the very expression of permanent discomfort. The corporatist system depends upon the citizen's desire for inner comfort. Equilibrium is dependent upon our recognition of reality, which is the acceptance of permanent psychic discomfort. And the acceptance of psychic discomfort is the acceptance of consciousness.

All Saints Island, 1995

NOTES

I—The Great Leap Backwards

1. John of Salisbury, *Policratus* (Oxford, 1909), vol. I, 19. CC.J. Webbs, ed.
2. Alessandro Manzoni, *The Betrothed* (London: Penguin Classics, 1972), 19.
3. Adam Smith, *An Inquiry into the Nature and the Wealth of Nations* (London: Penguin Classics, 1986), Books I-III, 421–431. First published in 1776.
4. Smith, 157.
5. Smith, 104.
6. John Keegan, *A History of Warfare* (Toronto: Vintage, 1994), 56.
7. Edward Luttwak, in an interview in *Le Monde*, 5 June 1995, 11.
8. Adam Smith, *An Inquiry into the Nature and the Wealth of Nations* (Indianapolis: Hackett Publishing Co., 1993), 178. This edition includes edited versions of Books IV and V.

9. "Heir to Italy's Revolution: The Irresistible Rise of Gianfranco Fini," *The European Magazine*, 24–30 August 1995.

10. *The Financial Times* (London), 22 May 1995, 6.

11. Emile Ajar (Romain Gary), *Pseudo*, Mercure de France.

12. Robert Grant, *Thinkers of Our Time: Oakeshott* (London: The Claridge Press, 1990), 15. The construct of these quotes is taken directly from Grant, an admirer of Oakeshott.

13. Grant, 62. Again the formulation is taken from Grant.

14. *Le Monde*, 24 February 1995.

15. *Harper's*, March 1995, 43–53.

16. Conversation with M. T. Kelly, June 1995.

17. Peter J. Williamson, *Corporatism in Perspective: An Introductory Guide to Corporatist Theory* (New York: Sage Publishers, 1989), 26.

18. Cicero, *De Legibas III*, 3.8, trans. C. W. Keyes, Loeb edition, 467.

19. Colin Morris, *The Discovery of the Individual, 1050–1200* (Toronto: University of Toronto Press, 1987). More than this quote, many of the attitudes expressed throughout these pages on the rebirth of the individual are drawn from this remarkable book. I would also recommend Walter Ullmann's *The Individual and Society in the Middle Ages*, although I differ somewhat with his interpretations of early individualism.

II—FROM PROPAGANDA TO LANGUAGE

1. James Hillman and Michael Ventura, *We've Had a Hundred Years of Psychotherapy—and the World's Getting Worse* (San Francisco: HarperCollins, 1992), 200.

2. Gordon A. Craig, *The Germans* (New York: A Meridian Book, 1991), 222.

3. Jean Lacouture, from a lecture at Massey College, Toronto, 22 November 1994.

4. Craig, 323.

5. Craig, 219.

6. *The International Herald Tribune*, 3–4 June 1995, 5.

7. Gustave Flaubert, *Dictionnaire des Idées Reçues et Maximes et Pensées* (Paris: Editions André Silvaire, 1991), 110. *"La censure quelle qu'elle soit me paraît une monstruosité, une chose pire que l'homicide; l'attentat contre la pensée est un crime de lèseâme. La mort de Socrate pèse encore sur le genre humain."*

8. Leonardo Sciascia, *Le Conseil d'Egypte* (Paris: Folio, 1983), 131. First Italian Edition—*Il Consiglio d'Egitto* (Torino: Einandi editore, 1963).

9. Anthony Storr, *The Essential Jung* (Princeton: Princeton University Press, 1983), 371.

10. Storr, 369.

11. Ivan Klima, *The Spirit of Prague* (London: Granta Books, 1994), 80.

12. James Hillman and Michael Ventura, *We've Had a Hundred Years of Psychotherapy—and Things Are Getting Worse* (San Francisco: HarperCollins, 1992).

13. Storr, 351.

14. Storr, 395.

15. Hillman, 103.

16. Homer, *The Iliad* (London: Penguin Classics, trans. by E. V. Kieu, 1977), 27, 130, 293, 320.

17. Storr, 123.

18. George Steiner, The F. E. Priestley Lectures, 1995, University College, University of Toronto.

19. Gregory Vlastos, *Socrates: Ironist and Moral Philosopher* (Cambridge: Cambridge University Press, 1992). All of these comparisons are drawn from Professor Vlastos' remarkable book. The summaries of those contrasts are in chapter 2. The breakdown of *The Republic*, in note 2.1.

20. Vlastos, 53.
21. Walter Ullmann, *The Individual and Society in the Middle Ages* (Baltimore: The Johns Hopkins Press, 1964), 102.
22. Government of Canada, *Canada in the World—Government Statement*, 1995, Ottawa.
23. Traute Rafalski, "Social Planning and Corporatism; Modernization Tendencies in Italian Fascism," *International Journal of Political Science*, spring 1988, 18(1), 10. The quote was taken from Paolo Ungari, *Alfredo Rocco e l'ideologia giuridica del fascismo* (Brescia, 1963).
24. The Nazi language examples are from chapter 14 of Gordon A. Craig, *The Germans.*
25. Denis Mack Smith, *Mussolini* (London: Paladin, 1983), 145, 28, 46.
26. Robert Owen, *A New View of Society and Other Writings* (London: Penguin Classics, 1991), 84.
27. Smith, *Wealth of Nations*, 120.
28. Craig, 105.
29. Jonathan Swift, *Gulliver's Travels into Several Remote Nations of the World* (London: Dent, 1894), 226.

III—FROM CORPORATISM TO DEMOCRACY

1. David Hume, *Theory of Politics.* Edited by Frederick Watkins (Nelson, 1951), 81. From *The Origin of Government*, the opening line of section VII, "Of the origin of Government . . ."
2. Nicholas Phillipson, *Hume* (London: Weidenfeld and Nicolson, 1989), 15.
3. Phillipson, 15.
4. Adam Smith, *The Wealth of Nations* (London: Penguin Books, 1986), 169.
5. Smith, 200.
6. Colin Morris, 73.

7. Walter Ullmann, 34.

8. Ullmann, 56–57.

9. Ullmann, 133.

10. *The Monastic Theology of Aelred of Rievaulx: An Experimental Theology.* Translated by Columban Heaney, O.C.S.O. Introduction by Thomas Merton. Cistercian Publications, Spencer, Mass., 1969, 144.

11. Ullmann, 137.

12. Timothy Kaufman-Osborn, "Émile Durkheim and the Science of Corporatism," *Political Theory,* vol. 14, no. 4, November 1986.

13. Robert Grant, *Thinkers of Our Time: Oakeshott* (London: The Claridge Press, 1990), 73.

14. Peter F. Drucker, "Really Reinventing Government," *The Atlantic Monthly,* February 1993, 61.

15. *Le Monde,* 9 June 1993. Monsieur Claude Silberzahn. *"La quête extraordinaire et effrénée de l'argent sous toutes ses formes . . . la corruption des élites . . . les classes dominantes de la politique et de l'économie dans une large partie du monde pour lesquelles l'argent n'a pas d'odeur."*

16. Kaufman-Osborn, 640 and 653.

17. Traute Rafalski.

18. Philippe C. Schmitter, "Still the Century of Corporatism?" *Review of Politics,* vol. 36, no. 1, 1974, 85.

19. Werner Abelshauser, "The First Post-Liberal Nation: Stages in the Development of Modern Corporatism in Germany," *European History Quarterly,* vol. 4, no. 3, July 1984, 293.

20. Denis Mack Smith, *Mussolini* (London: Paladin, 1983), 95.

21. Anthony Storr, *The Essential Jung* (Princeton: Princeton University Press, 1983), 377.

22. Gustave Flaubert, *Dictionnaire des Idées Reçues et Maximes et Pensées* (Paris: Editions André Silvaire, 1991), 145.

23. *Times Literary Supplement,* 16 February 1995, 25.

24. *The Globe and Mail*, 10 January 1993, A12.

25. Christopher Hill, *God's Englishman* (London: Weidenfeld and Nicolson, 1970), 104.

26. Léon Courville, *Piloter dans la Tempête* (Montréal: Québec/Amérique, 1994), 33 and 38.

27. Robert S. McNamara, *In Retrospect: The Tragedy and Lessons of Vietnam* (New York: Times Books, 1995), 6.

28. Deborah Shapley, *Promise and Power: The Life and Times of Robert McNamara* (Boston: Little, Brown, 1993), 408.

29. Shapley, 513.

30. Robert Owen, 55

31. Gordon A. Craig, 232.

32. Shapley, 143.

33. *The Globe and Mail*, 15 August 1995, A9.

34. Drucker, 49.

35. Plato, *The Last Days of Socrates* (London: Penguin Classics, 1975), 73.

36. Captain Joshua Slocum, *Sailing Alone Around the World* (New York: Sheridan House, 1993). Reprint of original edition of 1899. Born in Nova Scotia, settled in Massachusetts, Captain Slocum, in his 37-foot boat, took three years—1895–1898—to circle the world.

37. *Harper's*, March 1995, 49.

38. *The European*, 10–16 August 1995, 11.

39. Sylvester Stallone, *Tribute* magazine, summer 1995.

40. Mack Smith, 29.

41. George Grant, *Technology and Empire: Perspectives on North America* (Toronto: House of Anansi, 1969), 46.

42. Alvin and Heidi Toffler, *Creating a New Civilization: The Politics of the Third World* (Atlanta: Turner Publishing, Inc., 1995). Foreword by Newt Gingrich. Quotes are from pages 92, 94 and 101.

43. William Pitt, House of Commons, 18 November 1783.

IV—FROM MANAGERS AND SPECULATORS TO GROWTH

1. Robert Owen, op. cit., 96–97.

2. *McCall's Magazine*, November 1929, 18. "What's Right with America?"

3. Bank for International Settlements, 60th Annual Report, Basel, 11 June 1990.

4. Courville, 31. *"Une science, la gestion? Mais non, tout juste un ramassis de méthodes qui ont fait recette pendant quelques années d'abondance et de croissance économique. Maintenant, les recettes sont désuètes et les entreprises qui s'obstineront à les suivre disparaîtrant."* The school reference is on page 37.

5. Smith, *An Inquiry*, 152 and 437.

6. Cromwell, op. cit., 234.

7. Gregory J. Millman, *The Vandal's Crown* (New York: The Free Press), 107.

8. Elton, *Reformation Europe*. For example, see pages 233, 234 and 311.

9. *The Prague Post*, 31 May 1995, 7. "U.S. Economic Theorist Tells Central Europe How It's Done."

10. *Le Monde*, 16 May 1995, 4.

11. Robert Heilbroner, *Twenty-first Century Capitalism*, 1992 Massey Lectures (Toronto: House of Anansi, 1992), 87.

12. *The Toronto Star*, 24 August 1995, A10–A11.

13. Owen, XXVI.

14. Owen, 6.

15. Smith, *An Inquiry*, 200–201.

16. Homer, 304.

17. David Hume, "Of Commerce," in *Essays: Moral, Political and Literary* (Indianapolis: Liberty Classics, 1985), 266.

18. Bank for International Settlements, 63rd Annual Report, Basel, 14 June 1993, 218.

19. Smith, *An Inquiry*, 176, 181, 184. See also 183 and 201.

20. Michael Ignatieff, "On Civil Society," *Foreign Affairs,* March/April 1995, 130.

21. Millman, xi.

22. Hume, "Of Money," *Essays,* 281.

23. Smith, *An Inquiry,* 392.

V—FROM IDEOLOGY TOWARDS EQUILIBRIUM

1. Craig, 28.

2. *The International Herald Tribune,* 9 May 1994, 3.

3. Albert Camus, *Le Premier Homme* (Paris: Gallimard, 1994), 66.

4. Ullmann, 37.

5. Kaufman-Osborn, Durkheim article, 652.

6. The lightning examples are all drawn from a paper by the Nobel Laureate chemist, Dudley Herschbach, to the American Academy of Arts and Sciences, 12 January 1994.

7. Plato, *The Last Days of Socrates, 7.*

8. Ullmann, 124–127.

9. Storr, *Jung,* 394.

10. Durkheim, 649.

11. John Stuart Mill, *Autobiography; Collected Works,* vol. I, 233.

12. Giambattista Vico, *Vie de Giambattista Vico écrite par lui-même* (Paris: Grasset, 1981), 80. *Présentation par Alain Pons.*

13. Letter to Peter Carr, 19 August 1785. *The Life and Selected Writings of Thomas Jefferson* (New York: Modern Library, 1944), 373.

14. Speech in the House of Commons, 16 March 1886, in Oscar Douglas Skelton, *Life and Letters of Sir Wilfrid Laurier* (Toronto: Oxford University Press, 1921), 321.

ACKNOWLEDGEMENTS

My thanks to Bernie Lucht of the CBC for his support and to Philip Coulter for the multitude of skills he applied to the lecture series in all of its formats. To John Fraser, Master of Massey College, for his warm welcome and to Don Bastian at Anansi for his extremely helpful comments.

Many thanks to David Weiss for the originality of his energetic and persistent research; again to Laura Roebuck for her advice and organization; to Donya Peroff for rising efficiently to the stresses of time; to Bob Jacobs and Steve Boyd.

And, of course, to Adrienne.